The Racial Politics of **Militant** in Liverpool

The black community's struggle for participation in local politics 1980-1986

Liverpool Black Caucus

Merseyside Area Profile Group and Runnymede Trust
1986

Jointly published by:
Merseyside Area Profile Group,   The Runnymede Trust,
Department of Sociology,   178 North Gower Street,
University of Liverpool,   London NW1 2NB
Liverpool L69 2AF

ISBN O 902397 68 0

Cover design by Brian Thompson

Printed by Printfine Limited,
Gibraltar Row,
King Edward Industrial Estate,
Liverpool
L3 7HJ

Acknowledgements

This book has been produced by members of the Liverpool Black Caucus: Alex Bennett, Gideon Ben-Tovim, Clare Dove, Liz Drysdale, Steve French, Irene Loh Lynn, Ray Quarless, Protasia Torkington. The book has been edited by Gideon Ben-Tovim. It has been published with the help of a grant from Merseyside County Council, and produced as a joint venture between the Black Caucus, Merseyside Area Profile Group of the University of Liverpool Sociology Department, and the Runnymede Trust. We thank the various newspapers, NALGO, Merseyside Briefing, Merseyside Community Relations Council, Black Media Group, Black Sections National Committee, for the use of material from their publications. Some of the evidence given to the Labour Party National Inquiry into Liverpool District Labour Party has been incorporated into this book. Many thanks to Patricia McMillan for typing the manuscript. We should like, finally, to express our appreciation for the contribution made towards the struggles outlined in this book by all the other members involved in the Black Caucus since 1981, by members of the Black Caucus Support Group, by our friends and allies in the local black community, and by all those individuals and organisations both in Liverpool and elsewhere who have supported this struggle for racial equality and justice.

Liverpool Black Caucus,
September, 1986.

*"We are back in the world of dirty tricks . . .
I keep being surprised at how low the government
will sink to reach their nefarious goals".*

ARCHBISHOP TUTU

Contents

Contents

Foreword

The life of Liverpool's long-established black community has always been largely unrecognised by the majority of the white population. Although a series of reports has presented clear evidence of discrimination, the populace as a whole has remained steadfastly 'colour-blind', for the most part unmoved by obvious disadvantage and even unaware of the efforts of the leaders of the black community to achieve an effective equal opportunities policy in Liverpool.

The members of the Black Caucus who have produced this book have rendered their fellow-citizens a great service by providing this well-documented account of relationships with the Liverpool City Council and of events which have been hidden from the public eye. As far as we know the account of these events is a fair one. It merits widespread attention and whole-hearted response.

The appointment of Sampson Bond as Principal Race Relations Adviser became a well-known issue. The details of that appointment, which was clearly an affront to the local black community, are set out in their perspective in this book. The eye-witness account of what took place and the resolutions which followed speak for themselves and need to be known.

At the time we both felt that the appointment of a Militant Tendency black Londoner, with no real experience of Liverpool and its problems, to the City Council's post of Principal Race Relations Adviser, would undo years of patient attempts to build better relations between black Liverpudlians and the Town Hall. We therefore went at once to plead with the leaders of the City Council to reverse their decision, but in vain.

The tools of political power — like the advantage of patronage and the control of grants — were used to promote the Militant cause. For example, we were both present when the offer was made of fresh posts, with the necessary finance, for the Merseyside Community Relations Council in return for the recognition of Sam Bond. That such an offer was firmly rejected shows both the strength of feeling on this issue and also the solidarity of the local black community.

However, this book is much more than just the background story of Sam Bond. Here is a record of the long years of struggle to achieve the equal opportunities policy, the establishment of the Race Relations Liaison Committee, the shattering of the trust upon which collaboration had been begun and the attempt by Militant to introduce extraneous elements into Liverpool 8 to discredit local community leadership. Tragic in itself, the account contains many lessons which must be heeded by future administrations in this city.

This book is a sign of the steadiness of purpose of the Black Caucus and of the various groups its members represent. It is our hope and prayer that greater unity and a more co-operative spirit between the whole black community and the other parts of Liverpool's life may remove the long standing obstacles which have barred opportunities for so many black people in this city.

+**DEREK WORLOCK**   +**DAVID SHEPPARD**
ARCHBISHOP OF LIVERPOOL   BISHOP OF LIVERPOOL

Liverpool, August 1986

Preface

The Runnymede Trust is pleased to be associated with the publication of this study of recent political events in Liverpool for four reasons. First, the events it reveals have implications for the whole country, not just for the Labour Party or Militant, or the people of Liverpool. The authors draw attention, in their final chapter, to the dangers of 'colour-blindness' whether based on 'socialist, liberal or conservative principles', and the uselessness of relying on anti-racist rhetoric or an Equal Opportunity logo instead of using the substantial powers which local authorities have to bring about real changes. Everyone involved in local government, political parties and race relations in Britain can learn something from this study. Secondly, we welcome the opportunity to help publicise the experience and views of black and ethnic minority writers. We have already included in our Research Report on the Chinese community the views of the Chinese Information and Advice Centre in London and we hope, during the coming year, to prepare more publications by minority authors. Thirdly, we should like to see far more attention paid by the makers of national policy and opinion, who tend to be concentrated in London and the south of England, to what is thought, said and done in the rest of the country. Many people are aware of a crude North/South division, but it is essential to go beyond this and appreciate how much the distinct histories, traditions and present problems of a great number of living urban communities in this country are interwoven with the race question nationwide. The 'inner cities' have much in common with each other economically, but there is no single political or social pattern of an inner city, repeated like a stencil across the map. And fourthly, the city of Liverpool has a special significance: it has the oldest sizeable, settled African, South Asian and Chinese community in the country; and it was the first great English city to enter inexorable industrial decline, decades before the present recession. Other cities can learn from its experience in time to avoid what have proved to be mistaken or inadequate policies.

We wish to emphasise that the views expressed in this study are those of the authors and not necessarily of the Runnymede Trust.

Ann Dummett
Runnymede Trust, London
September, 1986

9

Introduction

The last two years in Liverpool have witnessed the most extraordinary events that must cause the deepest reflexion about the Labour Party, equal opportunity policies, the nature of racism and the range of oppressions facing Britain's black communities. There has been considerable national controversy over the role of Militant within the Labour Party, arising from Neil Kinnock's frontal assault on Militant at Labour's national conference in 1985. This story of the treatment by Militant of the black community in Liverpool and of the courageous resistance by that community against every possible form of oppression that Labour in office in Liverpool have brought against it, should provide perhaps the clearest available evidence for what Militant, when in control of a city council, really stands for.

This case study, then, should be of particular relevance and interest to all those who wish to gain a deeper understanding of Militant and its relationship with the Labour Party. However, Militant's approach to the issue of race is not unique: other sections of the Labour movement share a colour-blind, and purely class based analysis of racism that Militant has developed to extremes, so that this practical illustration of where this very vulgar 'Marxist' approach to race can lead to in the real world should be of far wider significance. The 'race/class' debate has raged for many years amongst theorists and political activists: when the revolutionary 'representatives' of the 'working-class movement' on Merseyside call in the police, to eject forcibly a group of black protestors (mainly women) who were trying to prevent Labour from abolishing at a stroke the democratically elected forum for the black community within the local council, then conventional formulations about racism and class struggle need to be closely examined.

However, still wider issues are thrown up by this analysis of the development and reversal of Liverpool's equal opportunity policies. Very little has been done in the five years since the adoption of an 'Equal Opportunity Policy' despite two years of Liberal office and three years of Labour control. This raises the broader question of racism in local government, involving not simply the commitment of the ruling political parties, but also the responsibility of council officers and of town hall trade unions: a mass of evidence about racial inequalities within City Council employment practices and service-delivery has been accumulated, the most serious street disturbances in Britain have occurred involving the local black community, constructive policies have been offered by local racial minority organisations for every sphere of Council action; and yet the clock has been allowed to be put back to before 1980 when the Council first agreed to adopt an Equal Opportunity Policy and to set up a Race Relations Liaison Committee to act as the forum for the black community to share responsibility for developing race equality policies and practices for the city. The Policy is now discredited, the Committee abolished, and the whole process has to be re-established: but the harm done to race relations in Liverpool and to the reputation of the Labour Party amongst the local black community, will take years to repair.

We hope that the publication of this book will help people to learn the hard lessons of these wasted years and to develop the determination to join with us to ensure that Liverpool's black community, the oldest and most oppressed in the country, as well as the most resilient, finally achieves the genuine equality of opportunity and of treatment that has been so vehemently denied by the current local Labour administration.

1 Liverpool in Context:
The Long History of British Racism

For a few weeks in the summer of 1981, the world's media focussed on Liverpool as sections of the black community were involved in some of the most serious civil disturbances experienced in mainland Britain. This was neither an isolated nor an unexpected phenomenon. In October, 1980, the Liverpool Black Organisation submitted a Memorandum to the Home Affairs Committee investigating *Racial Disadvantage* which indicated the long tradition of racism in Liverpool and warned the Committee of the consequences of further central and local government inaction.

> "Liverpool provides the best example of an old established black community, dating back at least as far as the slave trade. Many Liverpool streets are called after merchants who made their fortunes out of the slave trade. The present black community is largely the result of the union between African seamen and local white women. It dates back to the turn of the century when African seamen were employed as cheap labour by shipping companies trading with Africa. Despite the long established nature of the Liverpool black community, we feel in many ways further behind than black people in other parts of Britain.
>
> The Liverpool born black population is by far the largest of the racial minorities on Merseyside. Regardless of this we feel at best ignored by the authorities and at worst suffer all the effects of living in a racially prejudiced society. Our experiences as being an established British born black community here in Liverpool must be considered if the life-chances and opportunities for black people in Britain are to improve. What you see in Liverpool today is a sign of things to come; it provides a model for all major British cities with significant black populations, therefore, we feel that we must make ourselves clearly heard. In so doing we may avoid recurrence of the riots of 1919 and 1948 in this city, and Bristol 1980 and ensure that any future policies are aimed at finding the solution to institutionalised racism and the discrimination it engenders.
>
> There have been many reports, working parties, select committees etc., set up to examine the problems of black people. All confirm what we know at first hand, that black people are not treated as equals in British society."
> (Liverpool Black Organisation 1980).

The events, then, of 1981 need to be seen within a far deeper and longer historical perspective than is frequently the case, just as the whole analysis of British race relations should begin not with the experiences of the post-second war immigrants or settlers from the Caribbean or the Indian sub-continent, but with the experiences of the long-established Black British community of Liverpool. The false starting-point of immigration has encouraged British race relations studies and social policy to concentrate on issues of culture conflict, of ethnicity, of

13

problems of language and newness, rather than the central problem of racism which could not have been avoided if there had been public recognition of Liverpool's distinctive history.

One of the most extraordinary aspects of this history has in fact been the continued refusal of central and local government to take concerted action to deal with evidence of racism accumulated over this long period in Liverpool, so that it was not until the end of 1980 that some official local acknowledgement of the problem of racism was at last achieved.

Thus throughout this century, long before the sustained and violent disturbances of 1981, Liverpool's history has been punctuated by the periodic emergence of overt racial conflict and, of course, of black community resistance to oppression (Law 1981). In the summer of 1919, demobbed and unemployed soldiers led several days of violence against Liverpool's black and racially mixed households, culminating in the drowning of West Indian ship's fireman Charles Wootton (Julienne 1980).

Economic rivalry felt by unemployed and demobilised white ex-servicemen was one factor involved in the disturbances, whilst jealousy over sexual or marital relations between black men and white women (a central component in Britain's colonial heritage) was also very evident during these episodes: thus an "experienced police officer" told *The Guardian* (12 June 1919):

> "People here understand the Negro, they make allowances for his vanity and bragging. They wouldn't have been touched only for their relations with white women. This has caused the entire trouble. People don't like the marriage of black and white."

Such views were echoed in the moral homilies found in the *Times* or the *Daily Express* of the day:

> "A campaign of education should reveal to white women the well founded horror in which their intimacy with black men is held" (*Express* 14 June 1919).

The *Express* call to "remove the causes of inevitable offence" was followed up with moves to actually "repatriate" Africans resident in Liverpool. Indeed similar hostility to black-white inter-marriage, together with crude racist stereotypes of the children of these relationships — a substantial portion of the Liverpool-born black community — have persisted to the present day: thus a well publicised set of racist remarks attributed to the police and reproduced in the *Listener* in the late 1970s led to a militant response by the black community including a well attended march on the police headquarters and the local BBC station.

Storm over city race jibe by BBC

Black community groups have hit back angrily at claims that many "half-castes" in Liverpool 8 are the result of liaisons between black seamen and white prostitutes.

The allegation is made in an article in the BBC background magazine The Listener, written to link with the controversial "Merseybeat" television series about police work on Merseyside.

The article, by "Nationwide" reporter Martin Young, goes on to suggest that the youngsters are a problem with the law after growing up without a proper home life: "The negroes will not accept them as blacks and the whites just assume they are coloureds."

A member of the Liverpool 8 Action Group, Mrs. Paulette McCullinoch, described the article as deeply offensive to the city's black community and to women in general.

"It is just the old, old myth that any white woman who is interested in a black man automatically becomes a whore," she said.

The Liverpool 8 community had, by contrast, begged police to rid their streets of prostitutes and curb-crawling clients—all of whom came in from outside.

The article was also hammered by Liverpool council leader Councillor Trevor Jones, one of the fiercest critics of the "Merseybeat" series.

"People who have worked hard for community relations on Merseyside have a right to feel upset with the media for allowing this sort of ham-fisted and ill thought out use of wicked words," he said.

And the senior officer at the Merseyside Community Relations Council, Mr. Paul Sommerfield, accused the article of libelling a large group of people with untruths and misunderstandings.

A BBC spokesman said Mr. Young's view had been based entirely on what a police officer had told him: "It is obviously an indirect quote," he said.

A spokesman for Merseyside Police denied that police would give the "half-caste": "We would say people of mixed race," he said.

The article would be brought to the attention of the Chief Constable, Mr. Ken Oxford, he added.

BLACKLASH

BBC article sparks protest and threat of legal action

ANGRY Liverpool blacks are ready to take the BBC to court. They say a story in the BBC publication The Listener is untrue and will cause more trouble in the city.

And they warn people living in Liverpool 8 are condemned in The Listener as prostitutes and outcasts, say members of Merseyside Anti-racialist Alliance and Merseyside Community Relations Council.

Anger at the article erupted at a noisy protest meeting on Tuesday night when over 250 people decided to take legal advice on the report.

"They shows the disgust people have over the article," said David Clay, a community fieldworker in Toxteth who helped set up the meeting.

"The article seems to say that people here are prostitutes or outcasts.

"I am a product of a white mother and a black father. My mother was not a prostitute and my father was not even a sailor. The article is offensive," he said.

"It will cause more trouble. A lot of things have happened in the past in Liverpool 8 but it could get worse. Race relations in the city, if they ever existed, are deteriorating," he warned.

Mr. Clay also warned of a backlash against the police because of the article.

"Who gave the reporter the information? A lot of people believe it was the police and they will go even more against the police.

"They believe the police are like that anyway but now they have got it in writing," said Mr. Clay.

A demonstration is planned for tomorrow and hundreds of Toxteth people are expected to take to the streets in protest.

Police probe article

MERSEYSIDE Police have launched an investigation into remarks [...] made by [...] in a BBC reporter, it was reported last night. The police probe follows a call for an investigation by Merseyside Anti-racialist Alliance after a story by Martin Young in The Listener, a BBC publication.

The offending statements included a comment in which a [...] report that some so-called "half castes" in Liverpool 8 were the result of liaisons between black seamen and prostitutes.

---

rchers show anger at BBC's racist slur

bad weather more people, including city and trade union and [...] took part in a [...] centre of Liverpool [...] weekend to protest [...] racist slur" in the [...]ne. The Listener, [...] demanding that [...] should apologise and [...]ld indicate where [...]l came from was

handed in at BBC Radio Merseyside and Merseyside police headquarters.

Leaflets were distributed explaining that a whole community had been libelled by the use of such expressions as "half caste" and "the products of liaison between black seamen and white prostitutes."

The decision to call the march was taken at a meeting of the

Merseyside Anti-Racist Alliance, and local community and cultural groups, neighbourhood and welfare clubs, the Liverpool Trades Council, the Labour and Communist Parties and the Anti-Nazi League took part.

The chairman of MARA, Mr. [...] League said afterwards, "This march demonstrates the deep anger felt by the community at this racist attack."

Campaign on race slur

by David Utting

COMMUNITY groups in Liverpool 8 have launched an all-out campaign aimed at forcing the BBC to apologise over remarks claiming many city "half-castes" are the children of prostitutes.

A protest meeting has been arranged against remarks in the BBC journal The Listener by a reporter on the Merseybeat series about Liverpool police.

Mr Gideon Ben-Tovin, secretary of the Merseyside Anti-Racialist Alliance said last night that a petition

will also be raised against the article's "appalling" claims about "liaisons between black seamen and white prostitutes".

He said the petition would also be aimed at the Chief Constable of Merseyside, Mr Ken Oxford. "We want a full investigation into how police sources could have supplied such an untrue suggestion," he said.

And the multi-racial Rialto Neighbourhood Council [...] defied the BBC reporter to justify the claim.

"He knows nothing of

Liverpool 8, only what the police tell him," said chairman, Mrs Toni Warren.

Most prostitutes, she added, came into the area from the suburbs of Merseyside.

"They walk our lads' play streets plying their wares and then they return to their safe suburbia leaving behind their stamp of distaste," said Mrs Warren.

She argued all the [...] angered by the slur to attend the meeting on Tuesday night at the [...]oy House [...] centre.

Crackdown call on TV 'informers'

DISCIPLINARY action against Merseyside policemen, who "informed" on Liverpool's coloured community, has been called for.

There have already been complaints about remarks in a BBC magazine article on the controversial TV series, "Merseybeat", referring to "half-castes".

Today Liverpool City Council's Policy and Finance Committee will discuss two further complaints about the article, written by TV reporter Martin Young.

The leader of the City Council, Councillor Trevor Jones (Lib.) wants the committee to deplore the statements made both in print and on the TV programme about Liverpool 8.

And he wants Chief Constable Ken Oxford, to take appropriate disciplinary action against officers who issued the statements.

Councillor Cyril Carr (Lib.) also asks the committee to protest about the article in "The Listener".

He wants a public apology from the B.B.C. an investigation to the Chief Constable and a B.B.C. promise that a local committee can direct a TV film to give "a truer picture of the problems," in Liverpool 8.

Meanwhile the Lord [...]

Mayor of Liverpool (Councillor Mr. Ruth Dean) has written to "The Listener" registering "my strongest objection and indeed resignance for many generations Liverpool has welcomed men and women from all parts of the world who have made their homes in this City. They have brought with them from their own countries flavour of their own traditions and cultures which have greatly enriched Liverpool life.

The letter goes on: "It is essential that people from all races and backgrounds increasingly learn the secret of living together on a basis of mutual respect and appreciation of the part each has to play and the contribution each has to make to society as a whole. With its own traditions and background Liverpool can and does play its part in this learning process. The slur which you have published in the article about which I complain is on no view disgraceful and should be withdrawn quickly and publicly with due apology to those concerned."

Black

MERSEYSIDE Anti-Racialist Alliance is planning a demonstration tomorrow after comments in a recent BBC publication.

THEY'LL MARCH TO PROTEST

Those community, black and white leaders feel, have done a great deal to harm the goodwill being built up between the police and black communities.

The offending statements included a comment by reporter Martin Young in The Listener in which it was reported that many so-called "half castes" in Liverpool 8 are the result of liaisons between black men and white prostitutes.

A BBC spokesman claims that this and other comments had been based on a conversation with a police officer.

During the march, due to start at 11 a.m. from Stanley House, Upper Parliament Street, a petition will be delivered to Radio Merseyside offices calling for a public apology from the BBC and another will be taken to Merseyside police headquarters asking for an investigation.

Remarks 'deplorable'

"As well as this we are looking at the legal side of things with the possibility of making a complaint to the Press Council, said Mr Rashid Mufti, chairman of the Merseyside Anti-Racialist Alliance.

Mr Mufti questions whether the goodwill felt by black people towards the police force goes further than that between black community liaison officers and black community leaders.

"There is possibly goodwill at this level but I wonder whether it touches the community at a deeper level. I doubt if the antagonism felt by the community as a whole

has been dealt with," and these remarks reflect a symptom of something there all the time.

Another community leader supported these views when he said: "It is a very sensitive area and it has now been made difficult for people who have been working towards a better relationship. But the remarks do reflect the racist assumption which is still very apparent."

Mr John Hamilton, Labour leader of the City Council is also concerned a lot of the goodwill for the police will have been lost.

"Liverpool 8 does have a reputation for problems but it is not so much from the people who live there but from the prostitutes who come into it from other areas."

One distressed and angry man is Mr Sydney Moss, chairman of Merseyside police committee, who feels that the police force has an excellent relationship with black people.

"But if any group wishes to discuss with me, as chairman of the committee, ways and means to improve relations further I would be very willing to see them," he said.

"The remarks that were made were deplorable and the writer, Mr Young, should reveal who said them. I have no evidence to suggest the comments were made by a policeman. What one man utters should not be taken as the view of the committee or the police force."

After the 1919 events, more black people than white were arrested — a pattern repeated in well publicised racial incidents in 1942 and 1948 when white people again attacked the clubs, centres and homes of the black community in Liverpool and again the treatment of police and the courts was much harsher to the black victims than to the white aggressors, whilst the media portrayed the black community rather than white racism as "the problem".

The final major incidents involving sustained racial conflict in the period before 1981 occurred in 1972 when street-fighting with racial overtones emerged for several nights over the allocation of new council housing stock to black or racially-mixed families on the Falkner Estate in Liverpool 8. But in less dramatic ways, the black population of Liverpool has been continually subjected to incidents of racial violence, harassment and abuse.

These points of sharp conflict are, however, only the crudest manifestations of Liverpool's racist traditions: there had also been a constant stream of reports indicating the multiple disadvantages of Liverpool's black community, going back at least to the notorious Fletcher (1930) and more objective Caradog Jones (1940) report in the inter-war period, and the post-war academic studies by Richmond, Collins and Manley. In the more recent period, the report by the Liverpool Youth Organisation Committee (1969) *Special but not Separate* highlighted the problems of young black people especially in the employment field, showing in 1968 there were only 75 black workers amongst the 10,000 employees in 19 Liverpool stores; this report led to the formation of Liverpool's Community Relations Council in 1970. Studies from the Sociology Department at Liverpool University that were presented to the House of Commons Race Relations Select Committee pointed to problems in the field of policing and the courts, education and employment that faced the local black community (McNabb, 1969, Melish et al 1972, 1973); the Select Committee itself stated in 1973 that "Liverpool, for all its long experience with a mixed population, has left us with a profound sense of uneasiness". The *Annual Report of the Race Relations Board's North West Conciliation Committee* stressed in 1976 the "institutionalised and hardened patterns of discrimination and disadvantage" in Liverpool. The employment issue was emphasised by the Government's Inner Area Study in 1977 and South Liverpool Personnel's report on *Black Prospects* in 1978. Year after year the Annual Reports of the Liverpool (subsequently Merseyside) Community Relations Council (presided over by the Lord Mayor) reiterated the many facets of Liverpool's race problems.

The most comprehensive analysis of the multiple aspects of racism in Liverpool was provided in the evidence to the 1980 Home Affairs Committee by the Merseyside Area Profile Group, consisting of members of the Liverpool University Sociology Department working with local community organisations. The report referred to the . . .

> "interlocking and unique set of disadvantages facing the black community in Liverpool: thus problems of occupational discrimination and insecurity, educational under-achievement, residential segregation, mental stress, encounters with the police, media insensitivity and racist remarks or attacks combine to create an oppressing and alienating situation, which may in fact be deteriorating in the current economic and political climate."
> (Merseyside Area Profile Group 1980).

A brief look at these problem areas should help point to the massive historical neglect of Liverpool's black community by the statutory bodies, the enormous scale of compensatory action required to redress the balance of racial inequality and the scandalous inadequacy of the post 1980 political responses documented in later Chapters.

As we have indicated, the largest racial minority group in Liverpool consists of the many generations of Liverpool-born Blacks; amongst the other minorities, the Chinese community is the largest and itself stretches back over several generations (see Lynn, 1982, Craggs and Lynn, 1985). The most widely cited and officially accepted estimate of Liverpool's black population as a whole is that of the Merseyside Community Relations Council (MCRC).

Table 1: Liverpool's racial minority population

Liverpool-born Blacks	20,000
Chinese	8,000
South Asian	4,000
African	3,000
Caribbean	3,000
Somali and Arab	2,000
TOTAL	**40,000**

The black community, then, constitutes about 8% of Liverpool's total 500,000 population — and being a very long-standing part of Liverpool society should be well represented in the various local occupational strata, in a range of housing forms and locations and in receipt of council services and opportunities at least in proportion to its numbers. But racism in all its many forms, overt and covert, conscious and unconscious, direct and indirect, personal and structural, has led to a situation of the deepest inequality, exclusion and alienation of the black community from mainstream institutions.

Thus, discrimination in the employment field has always been very intense with unemployment amongst young black people at 60-70% for many years and steadily increasing. This problem has not suddenly emerged with the slump in Britain and clearly will *not* automatically disappear with general economic improvement, contrary to what a simplistic race/class equation would suggest. There are few Liverpool born black people in professional or white collar fields of work, few skilled manual workers, few even in routine jobs in shops and offices. All available studies indicated the same figures in the period up to 1980 and, as we shall see later, they remained constant in 1986: a black population constituting 8% of the city, yet having less than 1% of the jobs with the City Council, and less than 1% of opportunities with city centre employers and stores (Merseyside Community Relations Council, 1986). Indeed, it is a community that has been without work for several generations (Brown, 1983) and that as a result of overt and institutionalised racism has hardly been able to penetrate any layers within the local occupational structure.

This has been reflected in the significant absence of black people from positions of responsibility in the labour movement, with few black delegates to the Liverpool Trades Council and hardly any black trade union officials or Labour councillors in Liverpool's long black history (though Liverpool-born Black John Archer became Britain's first black mayor in Battersea in 1919, and was a leading Pan-Africanist and international socialist — see Fryer 1984). In broad terms, the trade union movement has historically colluded in the third class economic status assigned to the black community, from their earlier efforts to undermine the position of black sea-men and to prevent black people working on public transport, though there has been some improvement in recent years.

As well as occupational marginalisation, there has been a long process of segregation in the housing field: the black community has remained near to the original docklands area of settlement in Liverpool, frequently in poor quality council housing, in an area with a social stigma for crime and vice. Considerable evidence was available by the end of the 1970s (confirmed in the 1985 CRE study) that black people have been contained for generations in particular parts of Liverpool 8 through a combination of deliberate direction, routine procedures and stereotyped assumptions of the types and areas of housing that black and white people respectively prefer or will accept (see Figure 1).

Where black people do move out of the Liverpool 8 area or own a shop or restaurant in a white suburb, they are frequently subjected to harassment, vandalism, abuse, even physical attack, whether by neighbours, gangs of youths or fascist groupings: such cases were continually reported to the Community Relations Council since its foundation in 1970 and regularly revealed in their Annual Reports. This form of racism has meant that many areas of social space have been difficult for black people to enter: many clubs are known to operate a

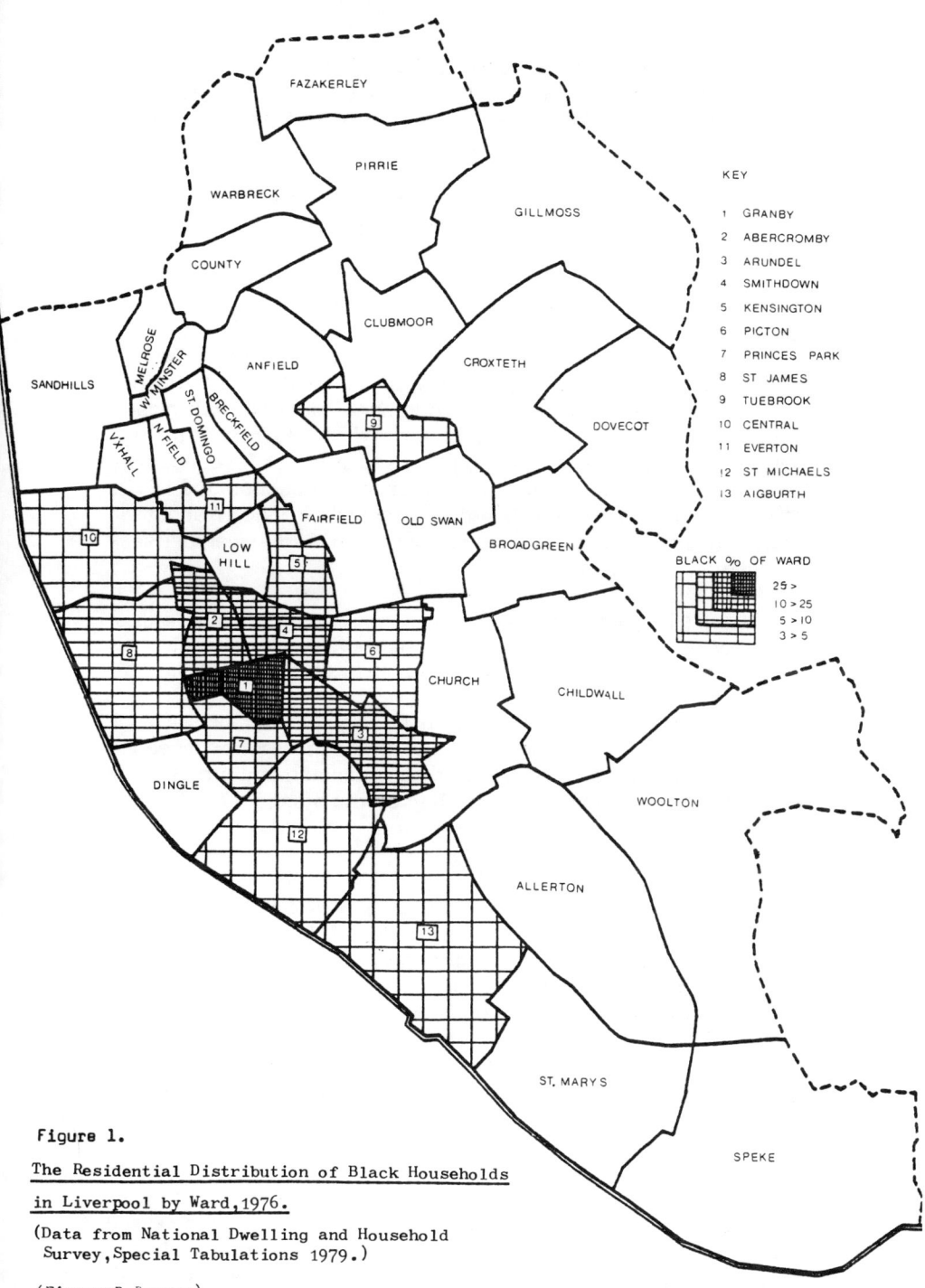

KEY

1 GRANBY
2 ABERCROMBY
3 ARUNDEL
4 SMITHDOWN
5 KENSINGTON
6 PICTON
7 PRINCES PARK
8 ST JAMES
9 TUEBROOK
10 CENTRAL
11 EVERTON
12 ST MICHAELS
13 AIGBURTH

BLACK % OF WARD

25 >
10 > 25
5 > 10
3 > 5

Figure 1.

The Residential Distribution of Black Households

in Liverpool by Ward, 1976.

(Data from National Dwelling and Household
Survey, Special Tabulations 1979.)

(Figure: B. Rooney)

19

'colour-bar', and many areas of Liverpool are felt to be out of bounds and a physical threat for black people. It has been widely rumoured that the burning down of the old Rialto dance-hall, notorious for excluding local black people, in the 1981 disturbances, was no coincidence.

A great deal of evidence was also accumulating that the social and health care services in Liverpool were failing to adequately meet the needs of the local minorities. Several reports in the mid and late '70s showed that practically no elderly black people received the normal social services available to elderly whites in the city and indeed in Liverpool 8: thus the uptake of home helps, meals on wheels, sheltered housing and day-centres by the long-established black population (and therefore with a considerable body of black elders) was practically nil (Merseyside CRC, 1980). Other issues such as the high number of black children in care, the lack of black foster-parents, the failure of the health service to meet black needs adequately, had also been raised as issues for concern by black organisations. With respect to education, throughout the 1970s black groups and parents had been expressing their concern about the low levels of attainment of the younger generation. As the Liverpool Black Organisation argued (op. cit.):

> "The failure of the education system in this city to meet the needs of black people has resulted in great wastages of talent and ability and has led to the frustration and alienation of many of our young people."

The system's failure could be seen in the very small numbers of black people entering further and higher education and those who succeeded in this way have tended to acquire their education and professional training as mature students rather than by the standard educational channels, or else by attending schools outside the Liverpool 8 area (Brown, 1986).

The most immediate form of oppression, however, for very many members of the community for at least a decade before the explosion of 1981 (see Melish et al, 1972, Humphrey, 1972) has been the police against whom allegations of verbal abuse, physical assault, continual stopping and searching, arrest and criminalisation on trivial or trumped up offences (threatening behaviour, breach of the peace, etc., drug planting) are found throughout the black community. There is no doubt that this long standing sense of grievance and injustice with respect to the police (whose patterns of arrest tend to be widely supported by the courts) lay behind the violence of the events in the summer of 1981.

There was available then through history, research and the struggles of black organisations and race relations pressure groups, generalised evidence to affirm the existence of racial inequality and injustice in Liverpool; yet local politicians, officials and trades unions persisted with

IS THERE A BRITISH COLOUR BAR?

Photographed by BERT HARDY

Britain stages Colonial Month—a campaign to stimulate popular interest in the life and people of the Colonies. The King attends the opening ceremony. But there are more than 20,000 Colonial people who live among us. What do we know of them—of their work, of their living conditions, their hopes and grievances? Picture Post conducts a survey into this dangerous and important question.

IT is not possible to find out the exact number of colonial coloured people in Great Britain. There is no registry of people with black skin, any more than there is a registry of people with black hair. And there you discover the first important fact about the colour bar in Britain : officially it does not exist. For the purpose of the law and the administration of Britain there is no distinction whatsoever made between white and coloured British subjects—they are all just British subjects. And the same official lack of discrimination is echoed categorically by all government departments, professional organisations and trade unions. But offices and organisations are run by human beings, and inside the minds of human beings, both in and outside offices, strange fogs of ignorance and prejudice can be at work.

Although there are no official figures, the coloured population of Great Britain is estimated by both the Colonial Office and the League of Coloured People at about 25,000, including students. This total is distributed over the whole of Britain, but there are two large concentrated communities : one of about 7,000 in the dock area of Cardiff round Loudoun Square, popularly known as 'Tiger Bay', and the other of about 8,000 in the shabby mid-nineteenth century residential South End of Liverpool. These came into existence largely as a result of the immigration of colonial coloured people to work as seamen, soldiers and factory hands in the First World War. They were supplemented during the Second. Smaller coloured communities are found in all the main ports including London (there is one of about 2,000 in North and South Shields), in Manchester and the industrial areas of the Midlands. The prosperity of these different communities varies.

The term 'colonial coloured people' is, of course,

On the Curb of a Liverpool Pavement a Coloured British Subject Expresses the Indignation of His People
Officially there is no colour bar in Britain. But from restaurant-keepers and landladies, employers and employees, even from the man in the street, says Nathaniel Ajayi, he and his people meet with considerable colour prejudice. Ajayi has lived in five European countries, was a British Prisoner-of-War in Germany, but says he knows of no European country where the coloured man is treated with more unofficial contempt than in Britain.

21

a steadfastly colour-blind and complacent outlook throughout the '50s, '60s and '70s.

Thus, as far back as 1951, the brief support that the Colonial People's Defence Association won from local Labour councillors in their campaign against discrimination in employment was over-turned as a result of trade union opposition (CPDA 1952). In 1969, Liverpool's Education Committee declined to accept the *Special but not Separate* Report despite the overwhelmingly establishment nature of the Working Party who produced the document. The Race Relations Board's strongly worded 1976 Annual Report was stridently attacked by Labour leader Bill Sefton as the product of interfering do-gooders and sensationalist sociologists. Again, as a result of intermittent representations made by local race agencies, particularly in the wake of the 1976 Race Relations Act, various ad hoc reports and resolutions related to equal opportunities were discussed in the Council, but always to no effect.

UNITE AGAINST RACISM!

WHO SAYS THERE IS NO DISCRIMINATION ON MERSEYSIDE?

* "Liverpool – for all its long experience with a mixed population – left us with a profound sense of uneasiness." – *Select Committee on Race Relations (1973)*

* "There is a kind of integration in Liverpool. But it is integration on the basis of inequality." – *Runnymede Trust (1976)*

* "Liverpool has still to recognise that within its boundaries an entire group of people, not immigrants, but black Liverpudlians, not only share the disadvantages felt by many white Liverpudlians but also suffer the additional disadvantages brought about by racial prejudice and discrimination." – *Race Relations Board Report (1976)*

* "Young blacks are growing up here with more stacked against them than in many other places because the position of blacks at the bottom of the pile has gone on longer." – *David Lane, Chairman Commission for Racial Equality (1978)*

MERSEYSIDE ANTI-RACIALIST ALLIANCE:

* Fights racist ideas, laws, propaganda and organisations.

* Investigates areas of racial discrimination.

* Promotes multi-racialism through cultural and social events.

Membership is £2 for organisations; 50p for individuals. Write to MARA, c/o Merseyside Community Relations Council, 64 Mount Pleasant, Liverpool L3 5SH.

ROOT OUT RACIALISM!

Liverpool's Chief Education Officer responded to the formation in 1978 of the Merseyside Anti-Racialist Alliance by writing a letter to the *Liverpool Echo* stating that "to allege racial discrimination is to incite discord" (MARA 1979); in a subsequent MARA public meeting he said that he "did not believe the system was any more rigged against blacks than against the Liverpool Irish, Welsh or Scots" (*Liverpool Echo,* 29 September 1978); such a refusal, however, to acknowledge the race issue was in total contradiction to the findings of the Education Committee's own three year Working Party on *Immigrant Children — Meeting their Needs* (1973-1976) which highlighted the special problems faced by Liverpool's black pupils. This colour-blind approach was reflected in two major local official planning documents produced in 1979, the *Merseyside Structure Plan* and the *First Partnership Programme Document* neither of which made any explicit reference to the particular needs and problems of racial minorities.

On the whole then, although there were occasional unsustained gestures by individual councillors resulting mainly from pressure by local race relations organisations, the majority of the key political actors maintained the position that an equal opportunity policy was not necessary, because the Council did not discriminate; that adopting such a policy could make race relations worse, by seeming to favour 'preferential treatment' for blacks and hence heightening sectarian divisions in a city which had a history of religious conflict; that anyway blacks did not have problems different from those of the rest of the working class/inner city residents, with the result that equal opportunities for racial minorities diverted energies and commitment from class struggles and urban issues and, finally, lack of support from the trade unions made the implementation of an equal opportunities approach impossible.

Thus there had been, by and large, an entrenched resistance to the formal and explicit adoption of positive race policy from politicians and officials alike. Whenever the issue was raised, it met the defensive response that the local authority's race record was good, as measured particularly in terms of the voluntary ethnic community centres funded under Urban Aid/Partnership, the Pakistan, Hindu, Caribbean and Chinese Centres.

Yet the overall ideological consensus to keep race off the political agenda did not prevent the uneven development of forms of action on race that were able to co-exist with official opposition to the possibility of such approaches.

As a result mainly of a joint approach from local race agencies for the local authority to make use of an Urban Programme circular to benefit the black community and, after the racial conflict on a new housing estate referred to above, a Black Social Workers' Project was set up within the Social Services Dpartment in 1975. This initiative had a problematic early history in terms of the management and organisation of the scheme and the recruitment and deployment of the workers. The project was originally described by the Authority as the 'Non-European Social Work Project' (in a city of third and fourth generation blacks!), and initially recruited immigrant graduates rather than locally born blacks (see Sommerfeld, 1979; Rooney, 1981). Again, in its initial period, it was operated within a firm ideology of 'integration' and with a conventional management structure so that for a while the project was simply used as extra conventional labour power to assist shortfalls within social services staffing. Nevertheless the scheme did represent a form of positive action with respect to the recruitment of unequalified black social workers and laid the foundation for later more progressive developments (Rooney, 1982, 1983).

Also within the Housing Department, an Ethnic Minorities Liaison Committee was set up in 1978 after negotiations between the CRE and the Liberal Chairman of the Housing Committee. This provided an official forum in which representatives of black organisations met with officers and councillors to discuss reports produced by the Merseyside Community Relations Council Housing Officer and to feed recommendations directly into the formal Council structures.

In addition, the Local Authority provided part of the funding for the Methodist Youth Centre, which catered almost exclusively for young black people and the associated 'Elimu Wa Nane' multi-racial education project; again through Urban Programme/Partnership sources, funding was granted to South Liverpool Personnel, the voluntary black employment agency and to the ethnic community centres; to the Authority's Multi-Racial Language/Education Centre and to the Charles Wootton Centre, a voluntary black further education project.

Thus some initiatives had been taken, but the general lack of acknowledgement paid to race both in terms of an absence of political will to develop overall race relations policies and the lack of a corporate local authority mechanism within which such policies could be developed, had the effect of keeping race projects and initiatives in the margins of local authority spending and service-delivery, and restricted responsibility for pursuing such developments to individual departments and committees within the authority. This is one factor accounting for the unevenness and incoherence of the initiatives that had been taken, and it also meant that a key official was in a position to ignore, defuse or sit on pressure from his Committee and local groups or organisations. The Ethnic Minorities Liaison Committee in Liverpool in fact met only four times in its first eighteen months and its existence was not even mentioned by the Housing Department in its evidence to the Select Committee in 1980.

The Authority had also failed to develop the Race Relations Working Party set up in 1979 under Partnership. The forum (which included officials, black group representatives, Home Office and Department of Environment and other local statutory advisers) met only three times and, at each meeting, the local authority officers put the onus on the black groups to produce detailed policy materials and took no initiatives of their own. The lack of clear status, functions and direction of this group and the change in direction in the Partnership scheme that followed on from the change in Central Government in 1979 contributed to the demise of this forum, which disappeared along with all other mechanisms for popular involvement in Liverpool's Partnership initiative. In another case, the proposal from the Ethnic Minorities Liaison Committee in 1979 to set up a 'Working Party to Plan for a Multi-Racial Britain' was ''referred back'' successfully by members of the Labour Group in Liverpool with no discussion.

Despite some of the more positive developments, which generally represented an ad hoc, marginal, fragile and relatively inexpensive response to voluntary and community initiatives, there was in a general sense a firm reluctance to move away from the official colour-blindness on race and to embark on a programme of radical and mainstream change to bring about racial equality. This was clearly expressed during the visit to Liverpool, in October 1980, of the Parliamentary Home Affairs Sub-Committee on Race Relations and Immigration, investigating *Racial Disadvantage*. Thus the Chief Executive of Liverpool stated that:

> ''the Council would feel that to declare itself an equal opportunity authority would certainly imply or be taken as implying that it has not been an equal opportunity employer in the past; . . . the singling out of a part of (Liverpool's . . .) unemployed community for special treatment could lead to as much disharmony as harmony . . .''

This statement of the Chief Executive needs to be taken as a fair representation of the deeply rooted ideological resistance by the local political establishment to act on what has been proved to be a most blatantly clear cut situation of racial inequality. This resistance cut across political party lines, with Liverpool's Socialists ('left' and 'right' alike), Liberals and Conservatives proving themselves equally reluctant to take racially specific forms of positive action and to develop comprehensive race equality policies and programmes; it was manifested in the defensiveness of professional local government officials to external criticism; and it was sustained by the restrictive practices won by the trade union movement.

Thus the official race relations view of this period was accurately reflected in the editorial of the *Liverpool Daily Post* (24 November 1978).

"the situation in Liverpool is simply this. There is no racial problem. There are problems of unemployment, of crime, of hooliganism. They are problems which trouble both black and white alike."

This commonsense view, on the whole, predominated amongst councillors of all political persuasions and amongst local officials, despite the considerable evidence available of Liverpool's deep-seated problem of racial discrimination and disadvantage and despite the efforts of local race relations pressure groups to place the issue of race squarely on the political agenda.

City out in force to stop racism

Morning Star Reporter

TWO THOUSAND people marched through Liverpool at the weekend to oppose violence and discrimination against the city's black community.

They highlighted attacks by the National Front and British Movement on black inidividuals and community centres, police harassment of black youth, long-standing discrimination at work, and deportations of black immigrants from the city.

The march—called by Liverpool Trades Council, the Merseyside Anti-Racist Alliance, the Anti-Nazi League and the new group of young Liverpool-born black people, Liverpool Black Organisation—displayed strong union support.

Among the banners were several trades councils, and organisations of the TGWU, NUPE, GMWU, NALGO, UCATT, ASTMS, NUT and CPSA.

Local anti-racist and anti-nazi groups were also out in force along with ethnic minority organisations and a large contingent from the Liverpool Black Organisation.

The Women's Liberation Movement, Christians Against Racism, Merseyside Gay Movement and branches of the Labour Party, the Communist Party, Socialist Workers Party and other left-wing organisations were also represented.

In a rally at the Pier Head, Mr. Wally Brown from the Liverpool Black Organisation argued that major efforts had to be taken to deal with the problems of massive black youth unemployment of Liverpool, now standing at 50 per cent.

Other speakers were Barry Williams, president of the trades council; Eric Lynch, from the Merseyside Anti-Racist Alliance and a local black shop steward, Herbie Higgins from the Merseyside Caribbean Council, and Bob Waring, president of the Liverpool Labour Party.

GO.. GO.. GO.. WITH THE LBO

— LIVERPOOL BLACK ORGANISATION

Although, as we shall see, a formal change was shortly to occur in the Council's approach to the whole issue, the long tradition of colour-blind inaction on racial inequality — and hence collusion in racism — outlined in this Chapter was quick to re-establish itself, despite the continuing evidence of profound racial injustices that persisted during the 1980s.

2   Equal Opportunity Policy 1980-1983: Liberals in Office

THE ADOPTION OF THE EQUAL OPPORTUNITY POLICY

On the 9th of December, 1980, the Policy and Finance Committee passed a resolution which seemed at the time to be of quite historical significance:

> i)   This Committee agrees to adopt an Equal Opportunities Policy and instructs the Chief Executive to bring forward an Equal Opportunity Statement for consideration by this Committee;
>
> ii)   This Committee supports the establishment of a Liaison Committee comprising representatives of the black community and nine representatives of this Council (three members from each political party) to be appointed at the next meeting of the City Council with the following terms of reference-
>
> > a)   to consider what are the obstacles to the achievement of greater racial harmony in Liverpool;
> > b)   to examine ways in which the City Council's policies might be extended or altered so as to contribute further towards overcoming these obstacles;
> > c)   to suggest priorities in any development policy arising from such examinations; and
> > d)   to report from time to time with recommendations to the Policy and Finance Committee, the Merseyside Community Relations Council and other bodies as appropriate;
>
> iii)   the Liaison Committee consider, at its first meeting, the other suggestions put forward by the community groups.

(*Minutes* Liverpool City Council)

This decision was of particular significance because it resulted in a complete about turn in the way that politicians and officials had traditionally regarded issues of race in the city, which, as we have seen, had been of the no specific problem, colour-blind, complacent variety: whereas now there was an official acknowledgement, however clumsily expressed, that there may be problems of racial inequality; there was also now a forum provided in which, for the first time, there was the possibility of official access to the decision-making process for the black community. The issue of race was, at last, officially on the City Council agenda and, at least in formal terms, a structure for black political participation was created.

The climate had so changed that there was now agreement from all three political parties to adopt an equal opportunity policy as had been proposed in a letter sent on September 23rd, 1980, from 16 local black groups and agencies.

The full version of the letter sent to the City Council, which also included annexes concerning "details of proposals for an equal opportunity policy" and "indicators of racial discrimination and disadvantage in Liverpool" (Home Affairs Committee, 1980) is as follows:

EQUAL OPPORTUNITY LETTER SENT TO LIVERPOOL CITY COUNCIL FROM BLACK ORGANISATIONS

23rd September, 1980

Dear Mr. Egan

1976 Race Relations Act and Equal Opportunities Policy for Liverpool

We, the representatives of the major black and ethnic minority organisations and race relations agencies in Liverpool, are writing to express our concern to the Policy and Finance Committee that after four years the Liverpool City Council, unlike a number of Local Authorities throughout Britain, has still taken no explicit action to implement the 1976 Race Relations Act. Section 71 of this Act impresses upon every Local Authority the duty of "making appropriate arrangements" to secure (i) the elimination of unlawful discrimination and (ii) the promotion of equal opportunity.

Approaches have been made to the Council in the past urging adoption of a full Equal Opportunities Policy, but the issue has always been deferred in one way or another. Yet as we document below there is by now very clear evidence of long-standing and widespread disadvantage and under-achievement in the areas of housing, social services and education and there is also severe under-representation of the black population as employees of the Local Authority. Furthermore, one matter which delayed previous consideration is no longer relevant now that the CRE has published a Code of Practice approved by both the CBI and the TUC.

It is true that some piecemeal measures have been taken over the years to develop a few projects of benefit to the black community and to support ethnic minority community centres. But these have been of a very limited and 'ad hoc' nature and in no way amount to an overall strategic response to the pressing needs of the black community, or the Authority's obligations under the Act.

Our local experience indicates that urgent action needs to be taken to stem the feeling of alienation and even despair amongst the minority communities, especially the youth. It is essential for the future of good race relations in this city that the Liverpool City Council takes a clear public lead in demonstrating its commitment to ending the long history of deprivation and disadvantage facing the country's oldest black community.

So we come to you now as a unified expression of all groups in Liverpool concerned with black deprivation, asking you to put this letter to the Policy and Finance Committee and to secure a commitment to implementing a policy such as that outlined below. We wish to stress that this letter and the policies included in our requests are a consensus view arrived at after considerable discussion within black groups and agencies over several months.

1. Equal Opportunity Statement

A clear and unequivocal statement, properly publicised and used in job advertisements and official documents, that the Council does not and will not discriminate in any way on the basis of a person's race, colour, nationality or ethnic or national origins, in the provision of services or as an employer, and is committed to taking positive measures to ensure this policy is actively implemented.

2. Mechanisms for Implementation and Consultation

The creation of mechanisms to ensure the consideration of the practical impact of Council policies and practices on minority groups, and the active promotion of Equal Opportunity.

a) A Liaison Committee between the Council and the minority communities meeting once every cycle and reporting to Policy and Finance Committee.

b) The appointment of Race Relations Advisers at senior level in all the major Departments of the Authority (Education, Housing, Social Services and Personnel).

c) Training sessions for Council staff so that they better understand the impact of their work on, and the special problems of, minority groups.

3. Monitoring

The organisation of regular surveys of employment patterns and services take-up and provision in the Local Authority, to provide a data-base for effective monitoring to see what is happening in practice as regards equal opportunities. Statistically the most satisfactory base of monitoring would be personal records of ethnic origin. This, however, is a contentious issue and a matter of concern both in the black community and among politicians.

We, therefore, ask at this stage only for a commitment to anonymous surveys of matters of interest at any given moment (eg numbers of blacks employed, black children in care, blacks in school, blacks in housing, etc.) and **not** for permanent personalised record-keeping. Most important is that any monitoring process should take place in consultation with the black community.

Such a policy, made known to the black community of the city, would go a long way to counteracting the present feeling that because of prejudice and discrimination the Council has no interest in the special problems faced by black Liverpudlians. It would also ensure that the Council became actively involved in fighting the sort of conditions that lead to eruptions of racial tension such as those in Bristol a few months ago and in Liverpool in 1972.

If once the Council agreed in principle to a policy as outlined above we would be happy to co-operate in the wide-ranging consultation with the black community and Council trade unions which would need to follow in order to device the practical details of implementation. We look forward to a positive decision by the City Council.

This letter was signed by Wally Brown as Chairperson of Merseyside Community Relations Council on behalf of representatives of the following organisations:

AFRO-ASIAN-CARIBBEAN STANDING COMMITTEE
BLACK WORKERS ASSOCIATION
CHARLES WOOTTON CENTRE FOR ADULT EDUCATION
ELIMU-WA-NANE MULTI-RACIAL EDUCATION PROJECT
HINDU CULTURAL ORGANISATION
LIVERPOOL BLACK ORGANISATION
MERSEYSIDE AFRICAN COUNCIL
MERSEYSIDE ANTI-RACIALIST ALLIANCE
MERSEYSIDE BANGLADESH ASSOCIATION
MERSEYSIDE BENGALI ASSOCIATION
MERSEYSIDE CARIBBEAN COUNCIL
MERSEYSIDE CHINESE COMMUNITY SERVICES
MERSEYSIDE SOMALI COMMUNITY ASSOCIATION
PAKISTAN ASSOCIATION
PRINCES PARK METHODIST YOUTH CLUB
SOUTH LIVERPOOL PERSONNEL LIMITED

Various factors seem to have combined to achieve the successful outcome of this approach to the City Council (see Ben-Tovim et al 1986). There is a sense in which this letter was, in fact, the outcome of two years consistent campaigning by an alliance of community groups. The period between 1978 and 1980 had seen the emergence of two new campaigning bodies, the Liverpool Black Organisation and Merseyside Anti-Racialist Alliance, which had organised a number of public activities including marches, anti-racist festivals, meetings and production of leaflets and information material which had highlighted many aspects of racism in Liverpool and won some public support for anti-racist initiatives: these two new groups worked alongside the more established Community Relations Council and local black and ethnic minority groups in a range of high-profile activities. By September 1980, the relative coherence and unity of the local black and anti-racist movement was expressed in a letter which involved all the significant local organisations. The fact that the letter was signed by the newly elected Chairperson of Merseyside CRC who was already Chairperson of the Liverpool Black Organisation symbolised that the demands were being made by the whole community, including the most long-established, but traditionally most disenfranchised, Liverpool born black community.

The recent Parliamentary Select Committee visit to Liverpool in October 1980 might also have had some effect on altering the attitudes of officers and politicians, with the clearly expressed concern by the all-party Committee for Liverpool's lack of race initiatives and structures. The extensive statistical dossier produced for this committee by the Merseyside Area Profile Group on *Racial Disadvantage in Liverpool* (1980) provided irrefutable evidence of the need for specific and urgent local authority action. Considerable lobbying had taken place of the trade union movement and of all political parties to ensure that there would be unanimous support for the proposal for an Equal Opportunity Policy. By the time the crucial Policy and Finance Committee meeting took place, the Chief Executive himself had clearly decided that the time had come for some shift in the authority's position on the issue, and he recommended support for the Equal Opportunity proposal.

Thus on the day of the Policy and Finance Committee meeting, in front of a meeting packed with witnesses from local black community organisations, the Chairperson of MCRC was allowed to address the meeting, itself a rather unusual gesture, and there was all-party agreement to adopt the Equal Opportunity policy and to set up a Race Relations Liaison Committee. This decision, then, was brought about almost entirely by pressure from outside the formal political structures of local government: it was the black community and its supportive organisations that had brought about this policy change, through winning over a series of temporary allies in the trade union movement, the political parties and the council bureaucracy. But the long history of ideological opposition to the development of race-specific policies and practices and the lack of action taken by any of these other agencies other than simply to agree to the proposals and initiatives developed from outside by the black groups, indicated the potential fragility of the reform that had been achieved on this occasion. Subsequent developments indicated that though a spectacular victory seemed to have been won, the battle had hardly started.

THE ESTABLISHMENT OF THE RACE RELATIONS LIAISON COMMITTEE

Liverpool City Council's formal agreement to adopt an equal opportunity policy, though of great potential significance in terms of a definitive formal acknowledgement of the race issue in Liverpool and in terms of the possibility of resource allocation to the black community and their involvement in policy-making afforded by the Race Relations Liaison Committee, was clearly only a starting-point. From the outset, there was the danger that the Committee might function as an ineffective talking-shop in which the officers would stall or subvert policy whilst the politicians might indulge in rhetorical argument. There was the possibility of the minority representatives becoming co-opted token figures doing little to push for effective change or to really extend the democratic process; whilst the immensity and complexity of the task of unravelling many layers of discrimination and disadvantage, both direct and indirect, might make little impact on the existing local patterns of racial inequality. Hence the actual structure and composition of the Committee, its resources and methods of work, its exploitation by local organisations, and the development of the political and administrative will to make it an effective vehicle for change, were crucially important in determining whether the outcome of the initiative was to be a real advance or an ultimately empty gesture.

The structure of the Committee was suggested by the local authority in consultation with the MCRC. In addition to the 12 political representatives (4 from each party) and the 12 representatives of black organisations (to be appointed or elected through the Merseyside CRC), the Director of all the major service departments were expected to be in attendance; the local Joint Shop Stewards Committee shortly became entitled to send four non-voting representatives; the meetings were open to the public to observe; and it was established that the Committee would report once each Council cycle to the Policy and Finance Committee which was itself the most important Committee of the City Council. Thus in broad terms it appeared that the Race Relations Liaison Committee provided a forum that gave the black organisations scope for making a regular and effective impact within the City Council and, for the first time, a legitimate access to the formal decision-making process.

COUNCILLOR REPRESENTATION

In Liverpool where there had been a tradition of official complacency and relative inexperience in the area of race, it was likely that the determination and thrust of political leaders was going to be an important factor in the success of any initiative of this type. There were, however, obviously potential problems militating against this outcome, given a situation where political alliances were a necessary part of maintaining overall political control as no single party enjoyed an overall majority in the 1981-1983 period, with Liberals holding office only with Conservative support.

Councillor representation on the Committee was decided in three different ways. The Labour group appointed its chief or deputy spokesperson for each of the major services; the Liberals organised a small election amongst all who were interested; and the Conservative representatives volunteered.

32

This unevenness of the method of appointment of the Councillors soon proved to have serious repercussions for the status of the Committee. Only the Labour group involved its more senior members in the Committee; of these, the most vocal and influential were advocates of an intransigent, class-only approach to race policy and, as part of this workerist ideology, they opposed any explicit measures to progress towards racial equality or to 'compromise' with Liberals and Conservatives. The Liberal party's members were, on the whole, junior and inexperienced members of their group indicating a lack of priority and commitment towards the race issue shown by the Liberal leadership: their nominee for the Chair of the group was a newcomer to Liverpool and the City Council who was a member for an inner city, multi-racial ward only recently lost by from Labour to the Liberals and who had demonstrated his interest in race relations through his membership of Merseyside Anti-Racialist Alliance. His junior status was reflected in the fact that he was not a member of the City's influential Policy and Finance Committee to which the Race Relations Liaison Committee reported as an advisory body, and hence not in a position to argue at that level for the decisions of the Liaison Committee. The Conservative Party members again did not include their Leader or Deputy Leader and only one of their major service committee representatives. Thus the formal and personal composition of the Committee ensured from the very beginning that the deliberations and recommendations of this Committee would not necessarily be translated into support at higher levels of the City Council's Policy and Finance Committee and the Council itself and, on many occasions, decisions were overturned or lost within the more significant Council structures.

The uncertain position of the Committee was indicated by an early symbolic difficulty in which agreement was reached in the Liaison Committee that members of the black group should be able to see a range of Council/Committee papers in order to increase their knowledge of Council discussions. At a higher level this proposal was blocked and delayed (though eventually agreed first as an "experiment" and then as standard procedure) on account of "cost" and "administrative difficulties" in making such papers available.

Despite his enthusiasm and commitment, the Chairperson's relative lack of weight and influence within his Party and the Council generally, and the marginal position of many of the other political representatives, helped undermine many of the decisions reached by the Committee and, again, the normal absence of key individuals, eg Chair of the Policy and Finance, Education, Personnel, Social Services or Housing Committees also symbolised the lack of concern for the detailed control over the implementation of the Equal Opportunity policy within the Departments and opened the door for significant policy subversion, dilution or delay at officer level.

OFFICER REPRESENTATION

The Directors of all the major Departments were supposed to attend at the Liaison Committee, which was serviced as a whole from the Chief Executive's Department by one of his all-purpose assistants (Special Assignments Section) an officer close to the Chief Executive, but with no particular specialist expertise in race relations and with other duties to perform besides overseeing this Committee.

The Chief Executive himself took a close interest in the early work of the Committee and normally attended the meetings, and also organised occasional Directors' meetings to stimulate progress. Liverpool as an Authority, however, does not have a strong corporate management structure, but is organised around a series of independent, powerful and relatively unco-ordinated Departments, whose general unevenness was reflected in the involvement in the Liaison Committee. Thus, senior management in the Education and Housing Departments hardly ever attended the Liaison Committee meetings in this period, though the Director of Personnel and the Director of Social Services and the Community Liaison Officer were very consistent participants. This level of participation was reflected in the inordinate delays with which the Education Department responded to any requests for reports that were presented to it and the cursory quality of reports produced by the Housing Department. On the whole, the most pressing weakness of the officers' contribution, was that they were almost entirely *reactive* in character: very few independent initiatives were taken except in response to persistent probing and recommendations by the black representatives.

In terms of specific input from Departments of the Authority with respect to the original demands by the black group for specialist posts, monitoring and positive action, the initial reaction was slow if not negative. The Director of Personnel's view (later reversed) was that no specialist officer on Equal Opportunities was required in his Department and ethnic monitoring was also inadvisable at present "because many black people are opposed to it", whilst no positive employment initiatives were suggested despite the evidence of massive racial disadvantage. The Departments of Housing and Education made no immediate attempt to respond to the proposals for action suggested in a general way in the Area Profile of *Racial Disadvantage in Liverpool* which the black group had put forward as their initial set of proposals; whilst the Social Services Department made an early attempt (repeated on a number of occasions) to make an internal promotion (of a white officer) to a new post of Race Relations Adviser, to which the black group immediately responded sharply as contrary both to the spirit of the Equal Opportunity Policy and of the Liaison Committee itself in that this promotion had been attempted without seeking prior consultation with, or approval of, the Race Relations Liaison Committee.

This failure to consult was a recurring problem but through continual black pressure it became accepted that any matter relating to race relations should be referred for comment and advice by the Liaison Committee, though the Liaison Committee had no decision-making powers and it transpired that race-related matters had, as a matter of normal practice, to be seen by the relevant Council Committee or Sub-Committee *before* the Liaison Committee had access to them. So the genuine inclusion of black community representatives within the decision-making process, ie a degree of power-sharing, was an area of continuing struggle.

BLACK REPRESENTATION

A heavy burden then fell to the black representatives to attempt to develop policies and monitor their implementation within the context of a Committee whose members broadly lacked influence (Liberals and Conservatives) or commitment (Labour) and whose officers largely lacked the will or the expertise to take significant initiatives.

The issue of the 'representativeness' of the black representatives on the Liaison Committee has subsequently become a controversial issue but, in fact, the process was quite clear and straightforward. Two sessions were organised by the Merseyside Community Relations Council, as recommended by the City Council, to select the 12 minority group members who emerged through a process of election by representatives of the various organisations involved in the original submission to the Council. Thus, counter to later allegations, the members were selected by a form of democratic process involving all the major local black organisations and race relations agencies. It was accepted that the individuals elected in this way were on the committee not to 'represent' the particular groups of which they may have been members, but to try to ensure the views and experiences of the wider black community were reflected in this policy-making process. It was agreed, therefore, that the members should report back regularly to the wider group of minority organisations who appointed them, as well as having their own regular 'caucus' meetings at which to organise policy input and tactics — hence the emergence of the term 'the Black Caucus'. The co-ordination of the work was to be in the hands of MCRC with responsibility for convening the meetings, liaising with the local authority and servicing the Black Caucus members.

The group of Committee members who emerged in this way were, of course, not a complete reflexion of the local black and ethnic minority communities: the Liverpool-born black population was under-represented, there were hardly any women, there was no Chinese community representation; on the other hand, there was still a reasonably diverse group involved in the Committee and a spread of expertise in the fields of employment, housing and education. Most importantly, there was no challenge to the legitimacy of the membership of the Committee, either from the politicians (all three parties fully accepted the mechanism through which members had been elected) or from local black groups who refrained from any public attack on the composition of the committee even if their own particular group or interest was not directly represented.

For the Black Caucus, the strategic priority for the Liaison Committee was clear: to achieve consensus on a series of practical proposals that would make a reality of the equal opportunity declaration. A consensus approach was necessitated because of the existing balance of forces in the Council which meant that any policy had to achieve at least two party support for success, which in practical terms normally meant Liberal/Tory support; and given the relatively controversial nature of the issue, it was felt essential to try to achieve all-party support wherever possible, which was not easy given the very combative stance of the Labour members of the Committee.

The initial work of the Committee proceeded fairly smoothly: a formal Equal Opportunity statement was agreed, largely as a result of suggestions made by the black group, which was designed to lay the basis for more detailed practical initiatives to be developed later.

LIVERPOOL CITY COUNCIL — RACE RELATIONS EQUAL OPPORTUNITY STATEMENT

This City Council declares itself to be an Equal Opportunity Council and is determined that both in its provision of services and as an employer, it will ensure equality of opportunity for all persons regardless of race, colour, ethnic, or national origins.

As regards the provision of services such as education, housing and social services this means that the Council will take active steps to ensure that all requests for and recipients of any service are treated equally. Policies and procedures will be designed not to discriminate either intentionally or unintentionally against any group or individual. The Council will also seek to respond to any special needs experienced by particular groups.

As regards employment this principle will apply to the recruitment, training, pay, conditions of employment, work allocation and promotion of staff in all parts and every level of the Authority. The Council will also make use of the provisions of the 1976 Race Relations Act which allows for initiatives to encourage under-represented groups to apply for posts and for specific training facilities if members of an ethnic group appear to be unfairly concentrated in any one level.

It will also seek to apply these principles to all work undertaken for the Authority by external employers.

The Authority will ensure the implementation of this policy by monitoring the situation from time to time in consultation with the Council's Race Relations Liaison Committee and appropriate trade unions.

The City Council will promote, as envisaged in Section 71 of the Race Relations Act, good race relations between all persons of different racial groups within the City and will adopt policies that actively seek to encourage this.

After this statement was formally agreed, posters containing the announcement of the statement were jointly designed and distributed in public places, and the statement was printed on the pay-slip of all council employees. Internal staff training in the meaning of the Equal Opportunity Policy was set in motion. The results of the initial 'head-count' of all council employees, indicating the severe under-representation of black people in all layers of the Council, were also distributed and the need for employment initiatives was agreed in principle.

But in response to the ensuing lack of detailed and positive proposals from Council officials and politicians for further practical action, and the delays in response to simple requests and suggestions, the Black Caucus realised that progress was only likely to come through their own detailed input into the Committee, at least until such time as the Council had appointed a team of specialist race relations advisers and workers. They, therefore, began to produce a number of reports in the fields of social services, housing, education and other policy areas to supplement the *Area Profile*. They proposed a radical overhaul of the Black Social Work project; and submitted a very detailed paper on personnel and employment issues as the basis on which to mount concrete initiatives to promote greater equality of opportunity.

RACE RELATIONS LIAISON COMMITTEE
Report of the Black Organisations regarding Personnel and Employment Issues

Summary of Recommendations

1. *Target*
   Paragraph 2:- As guidelines for success of E.O. policy.
   — Aim to increase to at least 5-8% the black proportion of the Council's workforce — to reflect the local population mix.

2. *Special Initiatives to encourage Black Applications*
   Paragraph 3:- Extensive campaign to make E.O. policy known
   — Vacancy displays in community centres and agencies
   — Notify all vacancies to South Liverpool Personnel
   — Devise bulletin of vacancies
   — Utilise ethnic minority press
   — Identify categories of work in the Council where lack of blacks affects ability to respond to needs of black community
   — Ensure school careers officers are aware of E.O. policy and its implications.

37

3. *Review of Procedures*
   Paragraph 4:- With unions, review internal trawl procedures to obviate any possible indirect discriminatory effect.
   — Similarly, with respect to union nomination rights
   — Ensure blacks have fair chance to enter city's M.S.C. schemes
   — With respect to appointments procedures, ensure that all involved are aware of E.O. policy, devise mechanisms to monitor progress of black applicants, include candidates' commitment to E.O. as a criterion, consider black involvement in appointments to counter any single person's prejudices.
   — Develop grievance procedure for incidents with racial overtones among Council employees.

4. *Compensatory Action*
   Paragraph 5: Review qualification demands to ensure no unnecessary ones are blocking minority entrants
   — Develop 'access' programmes to assist blacks to achieve skill and qualification level where they can compete fairly with others
   — Review level of discretionary grants for F.E. studies
   — Include training component in any special projects
   — Review situation of present black employees to see whether any are held back unreasonably or for lack of training.

5. *Apprenticeship and Junior Entrants*
   Paragraph 6:- Urgent discussion with M.T.C. to ensure more young blacks enter apprenticeships
   — Review other Council entry routes for young people
   — Special campaign of liaison with secondary schools
   — Report from Careers Service on plans to develop actions in line with E.O. policy.

6. *Training of Council Employees and Members*
   Paragraph 7:- First priority for E.O. training should be
   a) Councillors and senior officers
   b) officers involved in recruitment
   c) officers in contact with black people. Departments to identify appropriate officers
   — Training seminars should last at least 2 days
   — Include race and E.O. sessions as regular component of all Council training
   — Unfreeze Public Education post at CRC to ensure professional input to E.O. training courses

7. *Monitoring*
   Paragraph 8:- Departments to provide quarterly returns of number of black employees
   — Immediate re-run of 'snap-shot' survey last undertaken in October 1980
   — Identify Council areas requiring detailed monitoring
   — Move to keep records of racial origin. As prelude, Director with CRC to prepare drafts of appropriate questions to demonstrate what is involved.

8. *Race Relations Unit*
   Paragraph 9:- Use Partnership or S.11 funds to create Race Relations Unit or specialist advisers including at least one on personnel matters.

9. *Other Employers*
Paragraph 10:- Council exhort other employers to adopt E.O. policies
— Use direct pressure where possible, for example, by insisting
contractors and tenderers must follow E.O.
— Join with County Council on Merseyside E.O. working party.

In addition to this comprehensive set of employment proposals, the
Caucus also produced a set of proposals for the development of multi-
racial education policy, in association with the MCRC Education Sub-
Committee. This initiative, again, became the basis of the formal policy
statement produced by the Council shortly before the Liberal administration finally fell in May 1983.

LIVERPOOL CITY COUNCIL POLICY STATEMENT ON MULTI-RACIAL, MULTI—CULTURAL EDUCATION

Part One — The Statement

The Liverpool Education Authority recognises and welcomes the
Liverpool Community as multi-racial, multi-cultural, multi-lingual and
multi-faith, and is committed to the promotion of equality of opportunity
for all and to the elimination of racial discrimination and disadvantage
within all the institutions it maintains. It therefore aims to extend the
principles and practice of multi-racial, multi-cultural education to all the
children, students and adults involved. To achieve this end, practical
consideration will continue to be given in all sectors of the service to
means to combat racism and to meet special needs. The authority further
recognises the necessity through the appointment and training of
specialist staff and in consultation with representatives of black and
ethnic minority communities, to frame appropriate courses of action.

The practical implications of this statement are set out in Part Two.

Part Two — The Practical Objectives

To promote Multi-Cultural Education for All
1.1   By requesting all schools, colleges and other centres to review the
multi-cultural content of their curricula and activities, to ensure that they
take into account the validity of black and ethnic experiences.
1.2   By monitoring the development of their work in this field following
guidelines established through consultation with L.E.A. and minority
group organisations.
1.3   By developing suitable resource materials with the help of teachers,
lecturers and workers in all sectors, within the Unit as outlined in 4.2
below.
1.4   By using available resources of the Liverpool black and ethnic
communities and generally supporting their self-help programmes.

To combat racism
2.1   By meeting the statutory requirements of the 1976 Race Relations
Act, specifically with regard to Section 71 of the Act requiring local
authorities to make it their duty —

a) to eliminate unlawful racial discrimination; and

b) to promote equality of opportunity and good relations between persons of different racial groups.

2.2 By eliminating racist attitudes in pupils and students through regular review of educational books, materials and resources along the guidelines laid down by the authority.

2.3 By seeking to recruit, train and promote black personnel and mount access programmes in line with the equal opportunity policy of the city.

2.4 By developing through in-service training, among not only teaching but also administrative and ancillary staff, a greater awareness of racism and an improved capacity to deal with its cause.

2.5 By producing, in line with the Local Education Authority's commitment, a Code of Practice to enable schools, colleges and other centres to take appropriate action in dealing with i) racial victimisation and ii) racist literature.

2.6 By continuous monitoring of policies and provision the Local Education Authority will collect information about its progress in promoting racial equality and evaluate its policies.

To meet Special Needs

3.1 By establishing a framework for regular consultation with representatives of black and ethnic minority organisations and race relations agencies.

3.2 By seeking accurate information about needs of black communities, including the monitoring of educational achievement and the take up of educational opportunities by ethnic minority groups.

3.3 By interpreting needs in the broadest sense, paying attention not only to children of statutory school age, but giving due weight to other sectors: pre-school, youth, post-school, careers, adult and continuing education.

3.4 By providing, for identifiable and separate ethnic educational needs with particular reference to the Liverpool-born blacks, for linguistic needs of communities both for English and Mother-tongue teaching and for educational implications of cultural and religious differences.

To provide Resources and Promote Action

4.1 By the allocation of funding for multi-racial education both from the Education Committee estimates and any additional resources.

4.2 By developing a suitably staffed and equipped Multi-Racial Education Unit to co-ordinate and manage the provision of multi-racial education, including the organisation of in-service training, the preparation of materials, the investigation of special needs and the production and monitoring of multi-racial education throughout the city.

4.3 By requesting staff and governing bodies of schools, colleges and other institutions to produce policy statements and programmes of action to promote multi-racial education to combat racism and meet special needs.

4.4 By establishing a permanent group consisting of representatives of the Merseyside Community Relations Council and other minority group organisations as well as education spokespersons and relevant officers to meet quarterly in order to review and advise on the practical implications of the policy statement and other common issues arising, and to report to the Education Committee on a regular basis.

Thus the energies of the Caucus members were soon fully occupied in helping produce a range of policy statements and in fighting for their adoption in the Liaison Committee. Involvement in the Committee became an extremely demanding commitment, with regular meetings in between formal Committees to plan strategy and tactics, to formulate policy and to write the reports. As a consequence the Caucus tended to work in relative isolation from other groups, in any formal organised sense, though members maintained their individual involvement in a range of community groups. Thus the extension of the democratic process beyond Committee members that was envisaged at the outset did not take place to any significant degree. This problem might have been resolved with further staffing or organisational resources to help service the Caucus, to facilitate policy-making and report-writing, and to ensure the development of a regular information service and consultative forum of black/ethnic minority representatives. But no resources whatsoever were made available to the Caucus or its constituent organisations and indeed the black groups and agencies were all to suffer from cuts.

THE 1981 'RIOTS' AND THE LIBERAL ATTACK ON BLACK ORGANISATIONS

We have suggested, so far, that the effectiveness of the Race Relations Liaison Committee in the 1981-1983 period was limited by a number of problems: the ambiguous status, functions and powers of the Committee manifested in the lack of involvement of senior members of the ruling party and the uneven commitment and participation of senior officials; the lack of adequate resources and structures to service the black groups and to help promote a consultative forum to advise or instruct the group members; and the failure of politicians and officials alike to take constructive action except after persistent pressure from the black representatives on the Committee. This lack of action was reflected in the tiny increase in the number of black workers within the City Council between October 1980 and September 1982 when a third head-count of the work force indicated that there were still only just over 250 black people out of 30,000 in the Council as opposed to an equivalent figure of 225, 2 years earlier (see Ben-Tovim, 1983).

Other political developments helped inhibit the taking of positive initiatives within the early life of the Equal Opportunity Policy. A protracted industrial dispute took place within the Liverpool City Council which meant that there were no meetings of the Liaison Committee between the 22nd May 1981 and the 5th February 1982, a period of nearly 9 months. This interval also coincided with the Liverpool 8 'riots' in July 1981 and the various activities and initiatives that immediately followed, eg the Scarman report, the Heseltine initiatives, the changed pattern of policing in Toxteth and the emergence of the Liverpool 8 Defence

LIVERPOOL 8
DEFENCE COMMITTEE

W H Y   O X F O R D   M U S T   G O

The call for the dismissal of the Chief Constable of Merseyside, Kenneth Gordon Oxford, has been made by the Liverpool 8 Defence Committee, the Liverpool Black Organisation and the Liverpool Trades Council, all of whom remain firmly convinced that he is the prime obstacle in the way of any constructive dialogue between the police and the community. Our specific reasons are as follows:

1. The responsibility for the fair and proper policing of any community lies with the Chief Constable. Oxford's own racism, combined with his belief that tough and repressive policing methods are the best way of keeping order, have resulted in excessive police harassment, especially of black people, which stretches back many years. Oxford must take the ultimate responsibility for this.

2. Oxford's own racism is an established fact. He is well-known for making derogatory and racist remarks about the Liverpool 8 community. Despite the fact that it has been pointed out to him time and time again that the term 'half-caste' is racist and insulting, he continues to use it in public and has even defended the use of the word. Oxford's own racism allows his officers to give expression to their racism and to indulge in the harassment of the black community. If the Chief Constable is a known racist, how can he be capable of stamping out racism in his own police force?

3. Oxford has shown himself to be incompetent as well as racist. His handling of the riots themselves led to a situation where he failed abysmally to maintain proper policing of the Lodge Lane area on the night of the 5/6 July 1981. His decision to use CS gas was taken without first consulting the Home Secretary or the Chairman of the Police Committee. The gas was fired without any warning, and the kind used was specifically prohibited for use in crowd control.

4. The treatment of those arrested during and since the riots is appalling. There is evidence of police beatings, ill-treatment while in custody, refusal of bail, and denial of access of parents to their children. Many have been in custody — some in prison — for periods of 2/3 weeks. We demand an immediate investigation into the treatment of those arrested.

5. In the 3 weeks that have elapsed since the riots, young people have been stopped and searched for no reason at all, racially abused and frequently questioned about their movements during the weekend of the riots. Many have been arrested and charged. The continued harassment of people on the streets is creating further resentment and frustration, and is leading to a situation which is dangerously explosive.

6. Oxford has now invited representatives of community groups to meet with him on August 3rd. This is a last ditch stand to gain credibility with the community. Does Oxford now believe that he can engage in dialogue with a community that has been harassed by his police for many years and towards which he has shown himself to be racist? The Liverpool 8 Defence Committee, the Liverpool Black Organisation, and the Charles Wootton Centre will be boycotting the meeting and call upon other community groups to do likewise ...

25 July 1981

Committee as a grouping that became particularly controversial through its attempt to force the resignation of Chief Constable Kenneth Oxford. This period was also one in which the unity of the black groups was fractured by a dispute that emerged between the Merseyside Caribbean Council and a group of locally born blacks over the use of the Caribbean Centre.

During this period, a further ingredient to the local community group situation emerged in the determined effort by the leaders of the Liberal and Conservative parties to make some small financial savings by denying local authority funding to those voluntary groups that were "not value for money" — which happened to coincide with those organisations which were at times critical of Liberal or Conservative policy and were, therefore, branded as being "in league with the Labour Party". A freeze on their annual grant and vacant posts hit the Merseyside CRC very severely from April 1981, when first the Public Education Officer and, later, the Asian Worker took up posts elsewhere. The actual amounts of savings were insignificant, as most of the funding came from Central Government anyway, under Urban Programme or Partnership, but every major black agency's budget and staffing were put in jeopardy in this period, particularly the Charles Wootton Centre, whose main dereliction was the fact that they had agreed to house in their basement the Liverpool 8 Defence Committee.

At a time when the City Council could have been expected to be developing a serious race relations policy both in relation to the Equal Opportunity statement and the severe disturbances of July 1981, the City Council leaders, particularly Sir Trevor Jones, the Liberal leader, were attacking those agencies that were simultaneously being relied upon to assist in the development and implementation of the Equal Opportunity Policy and to help retrieve the situation in Liverpool 8.

This response by the Leader of the City Council to the 1981 disturbances in Liverpool was matched by an equally inadequate reaction by the Labour leadership in Liverpool, which was keen to score points off both the national Conservative Government and the local Liberals, particularly with respect to the issue of unemployment, but showed no genuine concern for the grievances of the black community expressed in these events. Some of the Militant leadership attempted to set up a secretarian 'Defence Committee for Liverpool 8', led by themselves, involving the distribution of Labour party leaflets attacking central government policies and the proposal to hold a political meeting in the middle of the crisis, but they were soon seen off by local black community leaders. At the Council meeting held soon after the events, the MCRC Chairperson, Wally Brown, called on the political parties to cease their sectarian in-fighting and to attempt to take concerted action to deal with the many problems faced by Liverpool's black population, but very little of a constructive nature emerged from local government at this time. The Liberals' main initiative was to organise yet another survey of Liverpool 8 while Labour continually attempted to convert the issue into one concerning the Government's economic policies alone.

The Government's own response to Liverpool's crisis was also to turn the issue of race into the wider issue of the regeneration of Merseyside, under Michael Heseltine's all-white Task Force of imported civil servants and seconded local business executives, with the inevitable marginalisation of the concerns of the black community. Though local black organisations won support for a few of the ensuing projects (e.g. Charles Wootton Information and Technology Centre and Merseyside Skills Training positive action housing management scheme) they were being excluded from any meaningful access to the government's post-riot initiatives and resources (Task Force, Merseyside Development Corporation). As a result, there was no targeting mechanism to ensure main programmes and resources and new regeneration schemes were bent towards the black population. Grass-roots plans for an ambitious community-based and community-controlled Liverpool 8 economic development programme were refused, whilst the Government show-pieces of the Garden Festival and Albert Dock renewal were profoundly irrelevant to the black community — no attempt was even made to consciously use these schemes to employ or train local black people.

Only the churches emerged from the 1981 events with any increased credibility, through their efforts in working in close association with the local black community to help establish the Liverpool 8 Law Centre.

Other complicating factors emerged during this lengthy period when the Race Relations Liaison Committee was not itself meeting, but whilst public discussion and politicisation of race relations were enjoying a high profile through the utterances of politicians, police, church-leaders etc., and the various activities that took place in the wake of the July events.

LABOUR BREAKS THE CONSENSUS ON RACE

Firstly, a highly publicised political row blew up as a result of a motion passed at the Emergency Sub-Committee, the forum from which the affairs of the Liverpool City Council were managed during the dispute and from which the Labour Party normally abstained. As a result of a meeting between the MCRC leadership and the Leader of the Liberal Party at which the MCRC attempted to persuade the Leader to end the freeze on the MCRC posts, and those of other local race relations agencies and community projects, Sir Trevor Jones decided to put forward an ad hoc motion to the City Council on race relations to prove that, despite all outward appearances, he still did have some concern in this field. The ultimate motion was as follows:

> "That the race relations Liaison Committee be asked to examine ways in which the number of black persons in the Council's employment can be increased progressively so that the percentage employed becomes nearer to the percentage of black persons living in the Council's recruitment area".

This motion ought in fact to have been totally uncontroversial, since the Liaison Committee was already in the process of looking for ways to increase black employment within the Council and reports considering precisely this had been in preparation before the industrial dispute intervened. However, the Labour Party's spokesperson, leading Militant Tendency supporter, Cllr Derek Hatton, chose to oppose the motion and to put forward, with great heat and stridency, an amendment supported by the whole Labour group:

> "That the resolution of the Emergency Sub-Committee be not approved and in an attempt to increase the job opportunities for both white and black the moratorium on the filling of vacancies within the Authority be lifted and immediate discussion he held with the Local Authority trades unions as to how jobs could be created in order to improve the services of the City Council; full consultations would then take place with the black organisations in order to ensure that there would be no discrimination in the recruitment policy".
> (Liverpool City Council, December 18th, 1981).

Thus the Labour group made it clear that it was utterly opposed to any form of positive action on race that appeared to specifically benefit the black community. They argued that such action would exacerbate racism, by giving far-right groups ammunition with respect to "favouritism" towards black people. The Liberals counteracted by suggesting that the Labour group was itself fanning racist attitudes by publicly opposing compensatory action that was necessary to deal with the racial disadvantage faced by Liverpool's black population and, amidst accusation and counter-accusation of racism, the Lord Mayor had to adjourn the meeting for tempers to cool. With a great flare of local publicity, the political consensus on equal opportunities that the black groups had worked so hard over such a long period to achieve was finally shattered.

The Labour group's hostility to constructive race-related action did not, however, go unchallenged within the Labour Party as a whole on Merseyside. A condemnation of the Labour Councillors was moved, but overwhelmingly defeated, in the Liverpool District Labour Party, within which the Militant group normally had a political majority on most issues; whilst a motion supporting positive action was moved by NALGO members and won within the Liverpool Trades Council. This motion which was also publicised locally was then itself referred to the Race Relations Liaison Committee and was supported by the 4 non-voting Trade Union members.

The Militant group's ideological position with respect to race relations policy, ie opposition to any race-specific mechanism, resource or initiative in the name of "working-class unity", was reaffirmed by their supporters on a number of occasions after this, indicating an increasingly entrenched and assertive view on race within the Liverpool District Labour Party. This abrasively colourblind view prevailed at a Labour Party Policy Conference held to hammer out policy for the May 1982 District Council elections, at which the setting up of a District Labour Party Race Policy group was rejected. A similar argument was put forward by Labour Councillor, Tony Byrne, in the Housing Liaison Committee (Ethnic Minorities) to oppose a motion on the possibility of accommodation being provided for elderly Chinese (who were totally excluded from existing Council accommodation):

> "That this Working Party is of the opinion that hostels for the elderly should be provided to meet the needs of the local community as a whole and not for any particular ethnic group."
> (26th March, 1982 — Housing Liaison Committee, Ethnic Minorities).

The ethnic minority representatives in the Housing Liaison Committee put up a spirited reminder to that Committee of their earlier consensus on the necessity for forms of special provision, catering for members of ethnic groups with particular needs or disadvantages; and ultimately a proposal from a local Housing Association for permission to acquire property for Chinese tenants was, in fact, supported by the Liberal and Conservative spokesmen, with Labour abstaining. This episode was a clear demonstration of the ideological fragility on which the Equal Opportunity policy rested, despite the paper commitment of the policy, which had originally received all-Party support, to "respond to special needs of particular groups" as well as to develop special initiatives to counter under-representation of black people within the Council and to prevent indirect as well as direct forms of discrimination.

When the Committee reconvened and began to look closely at the detailed set of employment proposals the black group had prepared, the Labour Councillors on the Liaison Committee once again launched a major assault on the black group's suggestion that a broad target should be set for the level of black employment within the Council in line with the proportion of black people within the city: they were opposed to any form of "positive discrimination" in favour of Liverpool's black population; given Liverpool's current economic climate and the City Council's general cut-backs in services and jobs, they argued that "reverse discrimination" would encourage a "right-wing racist back-lash." The black group in turn vehemently attacked this view: the Labour Party was itself encouraging this form of reaction by its public and inflammatory articulation of this position, which was utterly irresponsible when the special problem of black under-representation within the Council's own work-force and local racial disadvantage had been so clearly demonstrated; they also stressed that what was being advocated at this stage was in fact not "reverse discrimination" but rather a series of proposals for "positive action" as allowed under the Race Relations Act and specified within the Council's own Equal Opportunity Policy.

This debate was bitterly argued between the Labour group on the one hand and the black group supported by the trade unionists on the other, with the Liberals and Conservatives on the whole being passive spectators. By the end of the discussion (which was in fact spread over three separate meetings held in rapid succession due to the back-log of work awaiting the Committee and the length of the black group's paper) despite Labour again warning of their total opposition to any form of ethnic record-keeping even though the black representatives themselves were advocating it, most of the employment package was, in fact, broadly accepted in principle to be followed by further reports from various Departments of the Local Authority.

CONCLUSION:
EQUAL OPPORTUNITY POLICIES AND THE POLITICS OF "TOYTOWN"

And so, despite fierce Labour opposition and lukewarm Liberal and Conservative support, demonstrating clearly the extraordinary ideological diversity and contradictions that can be subsumed within an 'Equal Opportunity' policy — especially with respect to 'positive action', paralleling national ambiguities here — some slow progress towards consolidating constructive initiatives was made: the Committee had agreed on a target (though no time-scale was specified), on the need to review recruitment in detail, including current internal trawl procedures which amounted to a form of indirect discrimination, special schemes to recruit more black apprentices and trainees, and monitoring through regular snap-shot surveys and possibly personalised record-keeping (the most contentious issue); also some moves to overhaul mainstream council service delivery in the fields of social services, education and housing were being taken.

Hence it had proved possible to use the forum, despite its structural limitations and ideological difficulties, to win consent for a set of more detailed policy recommendations that might give substance to the general Equal Opportunity commitment. On the other hand, it was also clear that existing will for initiating or implementing initiatives at Departmental level was sluggish and uneven, reflected in the very slow pace at which staffing and material resources were made available for the practical development of the policies agreed to within the Committee.

Departmental lack of commitment and unevenness were encouraged, as we have seen, by, on the one hand, the attack on the major local black and race relations agencies that had been launched by the Leader of the City Council and the generally low priority and lack of interest shown with respect to race related initiatives by the ruling Liberal group and, on the other, by the consistent opposition emerging from the Labour Party to constructive and specific race related measures. By the end of the 1981-1983 period, leading Labour Councillors added two new examples of opposition to 'positive discrimination' to the ones already outlined: they openly attacked a Social Services Department proposal for a specialist Chinese unit to deal with the particular problems of the Chinese community in Liverpool ("it must not be done at the expense of existing provision" Labour personnel spokesman, Derek Hatton, *Liverpool Echo* 8 April 1983) and also their housing spokesperson, Tony Byrne, articulated a dogmatic approach to dealing with cases of racial harassment on council housing estates (their policy, whilst in theory trying to move the perpetrators of racist attacks — a fine ideal — was in practice one of making the harassed tenants stick it out and of being obstructive in dealing with their requests to move into less threatening accommodation).

Some of the necessary ingredients then for the development of a serious Equal Opportunity Policy were slowly gathering in Liverpool: a policy statement, a city council sub-committee within which race policy could be discussed, an officer's working party to monitor progress, race relations training, the gradual appointment of a set of advisers, moves towards ethnic record-keeping and positive action programmes; yet on the whole, substantial steps to actually radically transform existing patterns of recruitment and to make real inroads into the massive black absence from the Council work-force or the inequalities in delivery and distribution of services, were extremely slow in developing. Despite having apparently pierced the former 'colour-blind' ideology and having forced race securely onto the political agenda by establishing a forum from within which race policy could be regularly pursued, the black groups still found massive obstacles both at Councillor and at officer level towards the development of constructive detailed practices to increase the proportion of black people within the Council and overhaul service provision.

In the whole 1981-1983 period, despite the wide public acknowledgement of the race issue particular in the wake of the Liverpool 8 riots and the official Equal Opportunity Policy that was declared before these events, the only section of the local authority to have made a substantial effort in the direction of employment and service-delivery initiatives was the Social Services Department. They had already initiated the black social worker project many years previously and during the current period proposed a new scheme for the large scale recruitment of black home helps within the urban programme, a new Chinese social work unit and a new post of Race Relations Training Officer. However in addition an Access to Higher Education course, providing an intensive Return to Study course for 20 mature black adults with four black lecturing staff, was set up in the Education Department, also with Partnership funding — and some new Section 11 posts were proposed at the end of this period for the Libraries, Housing and Education Departments when it became known that Section 11 criteria were changing to include Liverpool as a likely recipients of grant aid.

The absence of sustained political will, along with the general lack of imaginative and energetic initiatives at officer level, involved immense tasks for the black members of the Liaison Committee to both produce the detailed policy proposals that were not emerging from other sections of the Liaison Committee, to maintain their own internal unity and gain the external support of black groups in the city and to apply the same pressures on politicians, officers and trade unionists as had been proved necessary earlier in the struggle. Perhaps, not surprisingly, such a multiplicity of complex tasks was difficult to achieve — some detailed policy documents were produced and generally accepted, though implementation was consistently delayed; on the whole a united front within the Council chambers was maintained, but the delay in organising a form of wider group accountability had perhaps led to some loss of external support for the group as a whole.

With respect to the structural issue of access to Council decision-making, the opening had proved to be partial and insecure and yet continually available. A forum remained for Liverpool's black population in which pressure could still be legitimately and regularly applied for jointly planning concrete measures to increase opportunities for black employment within the City and to improve or develop services with respect to black/ethnic minority needs. As with the success of the initial Equal Opportunity campaign itself, once again it was the ability of the black group to make sustained and detailed interventions that had been the determining factor in any steps that had been taken towards substantial change: but it was clear that the possibility of sabotage of the Equal Opportunity policy by politicians and officials, whether by outright opposition or by more passive, delaying mechanisms, far outstripped the strength of the countervailing input that the black members of the Liaison Committee were able to apply, despite the general (though largely reactive) support they had received from the trade union representatives on the Committee, the Chairman of the Committee and the Chief Executive and his assistant.

Although the externally situated group was able to make a significant impact in terms of policy *formulation* nonetheless the group's impact on *implementation* was very limited without some kind of parallel energetic and purposive internal political will or allocation of substantial resources at officer level.

Liverpool's 'Toy-Town' political situation (as it was branded in this period), torn between an increasingly irrational, unprincipled and personalised style of political leadership by the Liberals, a marginal Conservative group and a fundamentalist and purely oppositionist workerism from the Militant-dominated Labour Party, proved unpromising soil from which a serious policy for increasing black employment opportunities and political power and improving service delivery to the black community could be developed, to say nothing of the obstacles deriving from Liverpool's general socio-economic problems (the growing haemorrhage of employment opportunities and central government resources) and the uncertain ideological atmosphere in the wake of the July 1981 'riots'.

So the Caucus felt that, in the absence of dramatic party political conversions, real progress would only come through the appointment of a very capable team of race relations officers securely established deep within the local authority as was happening in an increasing number of local authorities at the national level. Such a team, or unit, if it had the requisite status, location, staff and resources could provide the missing link of internal specialist knowledge and advice to officers and councillors, exclusive administrative responsibility and real commitment, and could act as an internal watch-dog for the official Equal Opportunity policy and a mechanism accountable to the black community for its detailed development.

It was clear from the 1981-1983 Liverpool experience that the adoption of an official Equal Opportunity policy and the development of new organisational mechanisms in terms of the Race Relations Liaison Committee and some individual Advisers, did not entail any lasting or deep ideological commitment to, or understanding of, the principles required to bring about meaningful change, particularly with respect to 'positive action' initiatives. The 'hung' Council in Liverpool had enabled some broad steps to be taken, thanks on the whole to a coalition of Liberal-Conservative support, achieved through the mobilisation of sections of the local black community and through the input of the black representatives on the Liaison Committee. The more clear-cut political situation into which Liverpool emerged with Labour's overall majority in May 1983, opened up a new chapter in which it remained to be seen whether in office the Labour Group would be as decisively opposed to any form of positive anti-racist initiative as it had been when in opposition.

3   Equal Opportunity Policy 1983-1984: Labour in Control

The election in May, 1983, of a Labour Council with a decisive political majority opened up a very new situation in Liverpool as, for the first time in a decade, one political party now had overall control. In terms of race relations, it afforded the opportunity to move beyond the implementation problems experienced in the 1981-1983 period as a result, at least in part, of the lack of a clear-cut political majority for the previous Liberal administration and the consequent considerable space for delay and subversion at officer level. On the other hand, the predominant political position of Labour Councillors who had so vociferously opposed positive race initiatives such as Derek Hatton, now the Council's Deputy Leader and Tony Byrne, now the Finance Chairman, presented a real potential threat to the gains that had been made, at least in policy terms, under the previous regime.

THE NEW RACE RELATIONS LIAISON COMMITTEE

The appointment of Derek Hatton to the post of Chairman of the Race Relations Liaison Committee was a clear indication of both the problem and the potential: his political influence indicated the possible significance of the Race Committee, but his earlier race relations record left the Caucus group with considerable misgivings. The appointment, however, of Tony Hood as his Vice-Chairman, gave the Caucus a little more confidence, as at that time Hood appeared to be a fairly sympathetic and reasonable non-Militant Labour Councillor and as a member for the multi-racial Abercromby ward had some apparent sensitivity and commitment on race issues (subsequently, however, Cllr Hood behaved no differently from his Militant colleagues, supporting the Bond appointment, the abolition of the Race Relations Committee and making no public protest at the Labour Group's manipulations and malpractices on the race issue and indeed on all other issues of Labour policy).

The composition of the Black Caucus side of the Race Relations Liaison Committee underwent some significant change too in this cycle. With the new municipal year, the outgoing black representatives produced their own end of term report and preparations were made for the election of a new group of delegates and, as had been formally agreed with the City Council and as happened on the previous occasion, the Merseyside Community Relations Council invited over 70 local Black organisations and race relations agencies to a meeting held at MCRC in July 1983, to select the group of representatives to take over from the Caucus members who had served during the 1981-1983 period.

51

The new Caucus membership contained many more women than before and also many more Liverpool born Blacks, Africans and Chinese: though there were fewer members of the Asian and Caribbean communities, nonetheless, a broad based membership emerged from this election and from the ad hoc elections that took place when members left the area or resigned for other reasons. Thus during the 1983-1985 period when the Council finally abolished the Race Relations Liaison Committee, the Caucus had consisted of representatives from nearly all of the major ethnic groups: of the 17 members who served in this period, there were 9 Liverpool Born Blacks, 3 Africans, 2 Asians, 2 Chinese and 1 Jew, with 7 women and 10 men: a fair reflection, on the whole, of the racial/ethnic composition of Liverpool's Black community with only the Caribbean community not directly represented.

However, the black membership of the Race Relations Liaison Committee was not there simply to reflect the different ethnic/racial minority groups as such: the new membership of the Caucus (who included several members of the earlier group as well) included individuals with a wide set of skills and experience, including active involvement in a range of local organisations and campaigns and expertise in many areas such as employment, housing, education and social services.

We have given a detailed analysis of the constitution and composition of the Committee because of the claims subsequently made that the Caucus was "unrepresentative" and "self-appointed". The 1983 membership, like the 1981 group, was set up by means of an open, demo-cratic process that was accessible to all local black and ethnic minority organisations and that had the full support of the Labour leadership of the Council. Indeed when a few individuals displaced from the earlier Caucus tried to complain about the composition of the Committee, they were very firmly rebuffed by the same Labour Council who later, after the Bond conflict in 1984, opportunistically reversed their stance and suddenly said the group was somehow not "representative" after all.

AN APPARENTLY CONSTRUCTIVE BEGINNING

The first few meetings of the new Race Relations Liaison Committee proceeded fairly harmoniously and it seemed that some practical progress was going to be made. Thus one of the first demands that the Caucus made of the new administration, the establishment of a central Race Relations Unit with a team of race advisers, met with a broadly favourable response. A sub-committee of the Race Relations Committee was established to look at various models of Race Relations Units in other parts of the country, and the issue seemed to be not whether such a Unit was necessary, but rather the technical questions of which Department it should be established in, how many workers were needed and so on. It seemed then, that an important concession had been won though, as we shall later see, the gain of the Race Relations Unit was turned against the black community by the crudely partisan nature of the appointment of a Militant supporter to the Unit.

In education too, it appeared that some movement was taking place. The black representatives presented a very detailed paper on the development of a Multi-Racial Education Unit (to be funded out of Section 11) which had been produced by the MCRC's Education Sub-Committee. This Unit would provide the resource base to begin to implement the Multi-Racial, Multi-Cultural Education Policy statement that had been issued, again through MCRC and Black Caucus pressure, by the out-going Liberal administration. Again the agreement in principle by the Labour leadership to most of what had been proposed by the black representatives seemed to be a significant break-through, in a city where the provision of resources to develop anti-racist curricular materials and training programmes were practically nil up to that point. The fact that it was the black group that was doing all the policy-development work was in itself an indictment of the lack of concern and commitment from within the Education Department and the Labour Group, but nonetheless the Caucus felt, once again, that progress was being made.

MULTI-RACIAL EDUCATION UNIT

Posts for the proposed Unit funded by Section II.

(i)   Head of Centre-Senior Teacher Scale.
Responsibility for the unit — expertise and experience in curriculum planning and the development of multiracial curriculum.
Knowledge of evaluation in education will be necessary, with particular awareness of ethnocentricity in curriculum and organisational structures.

(ii)   Curriculum Development Officers — Scale 3.
1 post Nursery/Infant, 1 post Junior, 2 posts Secondary.
Responsibility for multicultural curriculum development and preparation of resources, also assistance to be given to teachers to ensure use of materials in all areas of curriculum. Knowledge in detail of how teachers prepare curriculum in specified area.

(iii)   Training Officer — Scale 4.
Responsibility for the development of comprehensive in-service training, with particular emphasis on the use of experiential techniques for attitude change and the development of good practice. To ensure that teachers are made aware of relevant issues and develop appropriate skills.

(iv)   Special Needs Research Officer — Scale 3.
Responsibility for monitoring the implementation of the multi-cultural education policy and for the investigation of special needs in conjunction with the Multi-Racial Education Adviser in such areas as under-achievement, language, etc.

(v)   Home School Liaison Officers — Scale 2.
1 post Asian communities, 1 post Chinese community (existing)
1 post Afro-Caribbean/Liverpool Black communities.
Responsibility for the development of close home/school liaison with the relevant community, and for the development of projects to assist this liaison.

(vi)   Seconded Posts — Scale 2.
1 post Primary, 1 post Secondary.
One and two term secondments will be offered so that the unit remains firmly rooted in classroom practice and so that development in all disciplines can be assisted.

(vii)   Materials Development Officer — Scale 4.
Expertise in graphics and the various methods of production of materials in various media. Responsibility for technical assistance, particularly in relation to Curriculum Development Officers.

(vii)   Full-time Secretary.
To provide clerical support.

Other developments of a positive kind seemed to be taking place within the education sector. In association with the City's Multi-Racial Education Adviser and the MCRC, the Caucus had produced a Code of Practice on Racist Behaviour and Incidents in Schools and, once again, this received the agreement of the Labour Group and the Race Relations Liaison Committee. The Caucus again played a central role in production and presentation of a set of section 11 proposals for a race unit to work in the field of further and higher education, which were again approved of by the Race Committee.

ADVISER AND SUPPORT STAFF FOR MULTI-RACIAL FURTHER AND HIGHER EDUCATION

In order to try and eliminate racism from further and higher education establishments within Liverpool Education Department, to increase black access to these institutions, to monitor existing provision and investigate special needs, to develop in-service race relations training, to promote multi-racial curricula and resource-banks to develop special access courses and to support voluntary black educational and training initiatives, there is a need for:

(i)   *Adviser* for Multi-racial Education to co-ordinate this area of work throughout the Education system.
(ii)   *Training Officer*
(iii)   Multi-Racial *Curriculum Development*/Resources Officer (F.E. & H.E.)
(iv)   *Research Worker* (Special needs and monitoring).

These officers will work as a team, with a brief to cover the activities of the whole of the L.E.A. Further and Higher Education Sector.

Education officials at last decided to take some initiatives and they submitted some very bare proposals, with no prior consultation, on Section 11 posts for the Youth and Community Service and, here again, the Caucus were apparently able to exercise their power of veto with Labour support when they insisted that the proposal be not agreed until a genuine process of consultation had taken place with black groups in the community.

The Caucus had clearly learnt some of the lessons of the previous period and were using the Committee structure quite effectively to push policy through and to be vigilant towards attempts by officers or politicians to abuse the structures. They were also very concerned to keep the community better informed and involved than had been possible in the previous period and regular quarterly report back meetings were held to inform community organisations of progress in the Committee; a number of ad hoc meetings were called to discuss particular areas of policy; and active attempts were made to involve non-Caucus members in both internal Caucus meetings and in the public arena of the Race Relations Committee meetings. The MCRC's and Black Media Group's revamped newsletter *Black Linx* was also being used to give further public airing to the issues being raised in the Council structures.

In employment too, some slow movement seemed to be taking place. The proposal made in the previous Caucus group's lengthy employment document that training sessions should be extended from one to two days for all members of staff had finally been implemented, and the eventual programme involved a heavy input from Caucus and community members. The principle of ethnic monitoring of the workforce over which the Labour Group had shown a major resistance until now, was eventually established. Thus agreement was finally reached that there should be, in the first instance, point of entry monitoring of all job-applicants with a tear-off monitoring form.

A number of other specialist race relations posts, to be funded from Section 11, were also formally agreed and Home Office support granted: a specialist Area Community Liaison Officer, a team of three ethnic librarians, a team of four ethnic housing liaison officers, a Personnel and Social Services adviser, a Race Training officer in the Social Services Department, a central Race and Housing Unit. It was also agreed to explore the setting up of a Contract Compliance Unit.

Within the Social Services Department, again, several initiatives appeared to be taking place: a major report on the *Care of the Black Elderly* was requested by the black representatives and its proposals, including the establishment of a community hostel in Liverpool 8 were accepted; further resources for the Muslim Meals on Wheels service were agreed, progress in the establishment of the Chinese Social Work Unit seemed to be taking place, and reviews of the Black Social Work Project and the Black Home Help Scheme were set in motion.

Thus it seemed that progress was taking place on many fronts, with most of the issues that were raised by the Caucus leading to apparent agreement in principle: even in the Housing Department, controlled by Tony Byrne, who in opposition had expressed strong objections to racially specific schemes, the plans for the sheltered housing scheme targeted at black elders in the Liverpool 8 area were proceeding.

CRACKS IN THE CONSENSUS

However, it soon became apparent that this evident consensus was lulling the Caucus into an unfounded sense of security and a number of counter-vailing realities began to emerge.

A series of problems surfaced, mainly clustered around the Housing Department. Firstly, a dispute arose with respect to a request for the City Council to give support for the Merseyside Skills Training positive action training scheme mentioned above which would have involved the City providing placements for black housing management trainees, whose salaries would be paid by MSC. The Council refused to support the project, citing union problems over topping up the MSC wage to the Council's minimum level. In the Caucus' view, this prevarication was an excuse for an ideological resistance to the principle of positive action and the ease with which the Council organised its own general topped-up MSC Schemes (with no emphasis on black recruitment) proved the point.

Then difficulties were identified with the City's racial harassment policy which had been initially formulated through Black Caucus pressure. This approach laid the emphasis on removing the perpetrator of racist attacks rather than the victim, but its implementation was soon having the effect of forcing black families to remain in frequently dangerous situations, whilst the aggressors were not, in fact, caught or removed. Where the victims were finally allowed to be transferred, it was on a supposed 'like to like' basis which was applied in an insensitive and arbitrary way to move the families to most undesirable properties far from relatives and friends who might have provided the necessary support to these victims of frequently brutal racist attack. The Caucus attempted to institute a special Racial Harassment Working Party to review the policy but were consistently met by a resistance to such a race-specific mechanism and by the expressed conviction that black people were using the issue to "jump the queue."

The Caucus felt that the Labour Councillors were deliberately opposing practical measures to redress the balance of racial inequality and injustice particular where Cllr Tony Byrne and the Housing Department were involved. The preliminary findings of a Liverpool University study (financed by the Commission for Racial Equality) were revealed to the Race Relations Liaison Committee. The study, whose Steering Group was chaired by the City's Housing Manager, showed marked inequalities in the quality and location of Council Housing allocated to black tenants as compared to white: black tenants were housed in consistently poorer quality accommodation and were confined irrespective of choice to some particular parts of Liverpool 8 with no access to better quality, more suburban housing available in the South District under investigation (see Tables 2 and 3). Black people were totally excluded from sheltered accommodation and had encountered considerable problems of racism from Council staff and from some tenants, gangs of youth or police in their neighbourhoods.

Table 2   South City Allocations by Lettings: Potential and Average Quality

	WHITE	BLACK
Excellent (1)	38.0%	19.6%
Good (2)	20.0%	24.7%
Average (3)	24.7%	38.2%
Poor (4)	17.3%	17.6%
TOTAL	**100%**	**100%**
AVERAGE QUALITY	**2.6**	**3.2**

Table 3   South City Allocations by Location in Sub-Area of South City

AREA	WHITE	BLACK
Liverpool 7	16.7%	6.2%
Dingle	15.9%	2.0%
Brunswick	15.9%	4.1%
Aigburth	13.2%	1.5%
Lodge Lane	12.5%	10.3%
Granby/Falkner	10.9%	52.8%
Englefield Green	10.0%	15.9%
Liverpool 1	4.6%	5.4%
Princes Park	0.5%	
TOTAL	**100%**	**100%**

These were serious findings, based on an elaborate survey methodology, and corresponded to patterns of racial inequality in housing identified in other parts of the country. However, it soon emerged that the Council's leadership did not intend to act on most of the major recommendations, ie to institute ethnic record-keeping and monitoring of housing allocations; to increase black staff working in the Department; and to review allocations policy and practice in terms of the racial dimension.

So after many increasingly heated discussions, the Labour politicians maintained a principled opposition to monitoring, stating that "black people would not like it" despite the presence of the Black Caucus who were there as black representatives advocating this policy which was accepted by all local black organisations, and despite the fact that the two largest local housing associations had already been conducting ethnic monitoring with no objections from the black community.

Again, in terms of the staffing recommendations, the ideological opposition to the positive action housing management traineeships had already emerged; no steps were taken to fill the four ethnic housing liaison officer posts; a paper agreement that had been made to set up a race and housing unit was overturned, nominally because the principle of having a central race unit was being established and hence a specialised housing team would not be necessary.

And as for reviewing allocations policy and practice, the Labour leadership claimed that they were introducing a new policy that would eliminate any possibility of racial discrimination. Yet when the details of the new allocations system emerged, there was practically no reference to race within it and no mechanisms whatsoever were adopted to ensure the new system was monitored, to remove the sources of proven racial bias, or to redress the balance of proven racial inequality.

The final symbolic rejection of the report, whose methods and findings have never been challenged by the Labour leadership, came on the actual day of the publication (CRE 1984) when the Housing Manager responsible for the City Council's input to the Report was actually suspended from his post. The grounds for the officer's suspension and ultimate removal from his post (he remained on the Council pay-roll but with no work) has never been made clear in the nearly two years of this disciplinary action. No evidence has ever been formally brought against him, other than unsubstantiated allegations that he "intended to discriminate" against someone (presumably a Militant supporter).

This final incident should give further pause for thought for Labour members who have argued that the expulsion of Militant from the Labour Party went against "natural justice" and that Labour should not expel "good socialists". When in office these "good socialists" have established on this and many other occasions that they will not hesitate to use their power to crush opposition from political opponents, from employees or from voluntary groups in the most ruthless and undemocratic way, with no concern for established rules, procedures or the principles of "natural justice", as in the Housing Manager's case. His dismissal, sadly never seriously challenged by NALGO, was an act of sheer administrative abuse of power, to remove a senior officer who had merely been doing his job in an honest, professional and open-minded way and had proved, in the race relations field, not to be a pliant servant of the nepotistic and authoritarian policies and practices being imposed by the leading figures in the Labour Group.

A DIGRESSION: THE GROWTH OF MUNICIPAL STALINISM

It may be useful, at this point, to briefly consider some of the more general developments that were taking place in the City Council during this period. An enormous amount of political power was beginning to be concentrated in the hands of two Councillors: Derek Hatton, the real leader of the City Council (though in name John Hamilton was officially the Leader while Hatton was the Deputy) with particularly important control over all appointments in alliance with favoured union branches (of GMBATU and TGWU), and Tony Byrne, with total control being won by him over all financial decisions. This meant that every appointment had to receive Hatton's personal approval, while every financial transaction had ultimately to receive authority from Cllr Byrne.

These powers started to be used in an increasingly blatant way, to recruit personnel who would support the leadership, not just in general policy terms, but also with respect to loyalty to Militant or their allies within the District Labour Party. Particular loyalist enclaves were recruited, such as the Central Support Unit (set up as the Militant power house within the Council offices) and the Urban Regeneration Unit (set up as Tony Byrne's base from which to develop the city's ambitious house-building programme); a whole new loyal security force was also set up (which the local press have often called "Hatton's private army") under a new security chief whose appointment led to a storm of opposition criticism because of his alleged personal friendship with Hatton which was claimed to be his major qualification for the post. Apart from these "specialist" sets of political appointments (which the Liberals alleged were "jobs for the boys"), it is clear that control of appointments was becoming consistently used by the Labour leadership as a means of patronage to ensure political control and personal loyalty for Militant leaders and their allies: it was, as we shall see later, this blatant abuse of the power over appointments that became the basis for the major conflict with the black community.

Political acquiescence or support was sought, however, not simply from employees of the Council but from community groups. A series of problems began to emerge, not only because of allegations of "fixed" appointments, but through voluntary groups running into conflict with the Labour leadership over funding, planning permission, freezing of vacant posts and other such impediments. The Labour ruling core had little general sympathy for the voluntary sector, but these problems were faced particularly acutely if the voluntary group had displayed any kind of independence or critical stance towards the Labour leaderships; or if it had any involvement in the housing co-operative movement which was a particular anathema to Cllr Byrne, who held a rigidly dogmatic view that centralised municipal rented accommodation was the only acceptable form of housing that the Council would support. These narrow and sectarian political principles led to bitter conflicts with a growing number of community groups.

Firstly there was a major dispute with the St James Community Association which had developed an imaginative scheme that had won them substantial central government funding for a complex including a leisure centre and comprehensive health facilities in the Nile Street area. Unfortunately, Cllr Tony Byrne played an instrumental role in refusing to allow this scheme to be implemented, and despite enormous public protest to this arbitrary and irrational decision, the Labour Group as a whole, including Cllr Hood in whose deprived inner-city ward the scheme was based, ratified the refusal to give the appropriate planning permission required to enable these much needed facilities to be provided. No serious grounds were ever brought forward for jettisoning this scheme, which the Council eventually replaced with a smaller, more expensive health centre of their own.

This was only one of a number of occasions when the Labour leadership turned central government money away from the city — something to be borne in mind when finally evaluating Labour strategy for dealing with the genuine problem of inadequate levels of central funding and cuts in real levels of grants. It was widely suspected that the real reason for Labour opposition to the scheme was political sectarianism as local Communist Party members played an active role in the Community Association and in campaigning for the scheme.

A second well publicised conflict escalated through this period of Labour control over the attempt by Labour Party activists in the Vauxhall area to develop co-operative housing schemes (particularly through the Eldonian Association). Once again, control over finances and planning led the Council into increasing opposition to the efforts of local people to improve their housing conditions according to their own preference, ie for co-operatives. This resulted in the growing resolve of the Vauxhall Labour Party members to mount a concerted political opposition to the Militant Tendency, and in the virulent response by the Labour leadership to this threat by trying to dismiss their local working-class rivals as a "right wing Catholic mafia".

This extraordinary opposition to the housing co-operative movement has been a central component of the stunted vision of socialism displayed by Liverpool's Labour leadership. Rather than seeing co-operatives as an important strand of pluralist forms of socialist ownership with a fundamentally liberating potential of grass-roots democratic control, the Labour Party in Liverpool has allowed this popular development to be championed instead by the Liberals, the Conservative Government and the Prince of Wales. For the Militant leadership and their close ally, Tony Byrne, socialism is interpreted as the election of councillors to take decisions *for* the people, and principally to build centrally controlled council housing for them.

Within this paternalistic and authoritarian vision (normally associated with the right-wing of the Labour Party — but in fact uniting both the 'hard-left' and the right in a shared politics which combines the various strands of Labourism, Fabianism and Stalinism) there is no space for control from below as in the co-operative movement, or for the creativity or non-Party initiatives of the voluntary sector. It is the elected Councillors and the Party who have the mandate, and in between elections the people basically have no rights to comment or to criticise, and no role in participating in decision-making or in power-sharing, unless they are delegates to the District Labour Party (who agree with the Party line as handed to them by the leadership, that is: if they disagree or oppose the recommendations, they are "middle-class" or "right-wing").

RIVER AVON STREET CONFLICT

It was perhaps only a matter of time before this emergent style of tight and dogmatic political control over funding, appointments and Council powers would lead to a major clash with the black community. This came when Cllr Tony Byrne intervened to prevent the River Avon Street sheltered housing scheme from being implemented, which has clear parallels with the Nile Street and Vauxhall conflicts. A 75% grant from the Department of the Environment on a scheme with a total cost of £1.2 million had been secured for this project which would have provided sheltered accommodation for elderly members of ethnic minority groups who had, until then, been almost entirely excluded from access to Council sheltered accommodation and indeed from nearly all Council services. There were only 7 black elders in a total of 1143 units of accommodation for elderly people; and in Liverpool 8, there were only 9 black people receiving meals on wheels out of a total of 4,553, 6 black people out of 1,038 in day care facilities, and 8 black people in residential homes out of a total of 1,391 (*Care for the Elderly in Liverpool 8*, Director of Social Services, Liverpool City Council, 1983).

And yet, despite this scandalous proof of a situation of overwhelming racial inequality, the Labour Group refused to allow the scheme to go ahead, despite the proposal having been budgeted for, £100,000 in fees already having been paid, and all the various phases of planning, consultation and tendering having been completed. This led to a high

City Axes Elderly Housing Scheme –

The Government selected Liverpool - against competition from other cities in the country - for an innovation in sheltered housing, specifically designed for elderly members of racial minorities, who will live in a mixed community setting. The City Council has now changed its mind and is pulling out, in spite of the fact that the Government is willing to pay 75% of the cost. We need your support to fight to get the Council to change its mind again and provide this much-needed facility in River Avon Street, off Lodge Lane, Liverpool 8.

ABANDONED

Further information:
Community Relations Council
64 Mount Pleasant
Liverpool 3

Tel: 709 6858

profile "Save River Avon Street" campaign by the Black Caucus, the MCRC's Housing Sub-Committee and a number of local organisations, involving public meetings, petitions, leaflets, badges and so on, but with no effect other than to make it clear that individual councillors would take their resistance to any kind of positive action or special need initiative to the most doctrinaire limits. This clearly constitutes a form of persistent racism — a determined opposition to the taking of action on proven racial inequalities. It also transpired that there were at this time no reliable Labour City Councillors who would seriously oppose in public the will of the leading Militant axis; and Black Caucus representatives on the Race Relations Liaison Committee would not accept arbitrary and negative decisions without sharp public opposition, which included walking out of a meeting of the Race Relations Liaison Committee in protest at the Labour leadership's actions. The ingredients were being mixed for an even larger dispute between the Labour party and the black community.

The various areas of resistance that emerged in the housing field were only the most overt and clear-cut examples of what was developing as a consistent pattern of refusal by Labour's leading Councillors to support practical, constructive initiatives with an explicit commitment to positive action or meeting special needs of black/ethnic minority communities. The socialist colour-blindness that marked Labour in opposition was repeating itself with Labour in power, and most of the initiatives that were agreed at the beginning of the period in office started to be undermined or not implemented, though frequently this process of subversion of agreed policy took place behind the closed doors of the offices where real power lay, ie in the rooms of Cllrs Hatton or Byrne.

We have already seen how the agreed Section 11 posts for four ethnic housing liaison officers were not filled, as a result of the hostility of the leading politicians to racially specific appointments. A similar non-implementation of nearly all the other agreed Section 11 posts took place, despite having been formally agreed by the Race Relations Liaison Committee and Home Office agreement having been given to fund the posts at 75% level. The authority was not granted by Cllrs Byrne and Hatton to proceed to actually fill the posts for the ethnic librarian unit (3 staff), the multi-racial education unit (8 staff), the further education race unit (3 staff), the advisers in Social Services and Personnel, the race training officer in the Social Services Department, the Chinese social work unit (4 posts). Despite the potential importance of these posts in developing racial equality policies and practices within the various departments of the local authority, none of these have ever been filled, with the exception of the Chinese unit which was finally filled only much later in 1985 as part of the Labour leadership's attempt to find some support within the Chinese community.

Significantly the process of delay and non-implementation of policy was not now, as had at times happened under the Liberal regime, caused by the obstruction or lack of commitment of officers. The Labour administration displayed enormous political will for their own favoured schemes and priorities, which were introduced at breakneck speed, riding roughshod over political, trade union, community or officer opposition, as was seen in the speed with which they were prepared to re-organise the whole of the secondary sector of education (and later further education) and to introduce their programme of urban regeneration in a number of 'priority areas' (which largely avoided areas of major black concentration). So the failure to implement race related policy has to be explained on the grounds of the leading Labour Councillors' ideological hostility to all practical initiatives which would be of benefit to black communities, expressed in terms of preference for general "working class" initiatives and an opposition to "divisive" policies of "positive discrimination".

Once this clear cut political position was established, along with the expression of ruthless sanctions againt council officers who took up any kind of independent professional stance, then the 'normal' careerism and timidity of council officers not to court the displeasure of the ruling circle might have also played a role in the race relations paralysis that began to emerge under the new Labour regime.

In employment no steps were taken to introduce the Contracts Compliance Unit (and when this was finally introduced two years later in 1986, it was totally non-directive with respect to local contractors' equal opportunity policies). The commitment that had been reached with the Liberal regime to set a target for the employment of black employees within the city council of 7%, to parallel the size of the local black community, was declared to be unacceptable to the Labour rulers; although agreement was reached on some record-keeping for job applications, it was quite clear that the politicians regarded this as a thoroughly token exercise and no serious monitoring mechanisms or resources were made available.

A similar pattern of positive inaction or tokenism was emerging in other service areas too. In the Education Department, although a Code of Practice on combating racist incidents was agreed, it was not actually issued to the schools and colleges at all during this period and only finally brought back into the Council proceedings two years later, in December, 1985, and then with no consultation with community groups or trade unions.

As we have seen, the resource base necessary to implement the Multi-Cultural Education Policy, ie the units working in the schools and further education sectors, were not established (despite Home Office funding through Section 11); and the only practical response ultimately made to the issue of racism in schools, the establishment of Race Relations Co-ordinators in the re-organised comprehensives, was agreed only much later, again, in the summer of 1985, but without consultation with the black community, without adequate training, without resources or adequate job-descriptions, and as little more than a concession to the trade unions for more career posts which were only available to the existing pool of predominantly white teachers with little previous expertise in this field.

In the Social Services Department, no action was taken to implement the recommendations of the major report on *Care of the Black Elderly* and indeed, the agreement that a community hostel be built in Liverpool 8 was eventually removed from the budget, as usual by the discretionary powers of Cllr Byrne; and the Black Social Work project was ultimately allowed to be disbanded.

Finally, no steps were taken to establish the Central Race Relations Unit, despite various reports, trips to other authorities by the Sub-Committee of the Liaison Committee involving Caucus members, Councillors and Officers, and agreements on the desired shape and structure of the Unit.

By the end, then, of Labour's first year of office, the Black Caucus felt it necessary to re-evaluate their involvement in the Race Relations Liaison Committee, as it seemed clear that there was no commitment to implementing race equality measures and indeed an increasingly coherent pattern of active opposition to all initiatives that might have had some impact in transforming policies and practices in a non-racist direction. All that had been achieved was some high-profile gestures, in terms of the Council's sponsorship of the Chinese New Year celebrations (whilst delaying setting up the Chinese Social Work Unit) and its rhetorical opposition to the presence of fascist newspaper-sellers in the central shopping areas of the town centre, whilst in all areas of ongoing policy and practice, very little had been achieved and many set-backs had occurred. Even the training programme had been abandoned because of the refusal of the Council to take serious disciplinary measures against an employee who had been racially abusive to a Black Caucus member who was involved in the training process; this had led Caucus members and the Merseyside Community Relations Council to refuse to participate any further in this programme. One small concession was achieved at the end of this cycle, that is the agreement to allow the black organisations to be represented on all appointments to racially specific posts. This became significant over the subsequent struggle around the Principal Race Adviser post, but in the wake of that conflict this right was removed by the Labour leadership.

Given the overwhelmingly negative pattern that was becoming clearly identified, the Caucus resolved to begin the new cycle in June, 1984, with an ultimatum to the Labour leadership: either they would present to the Caucus a statement of policy that they were committed to positive and practical measures to eliminate racial equality, or the Caucus would resign from the Committee. Caucus members also withdrew from a Council 'Anti-Racist Campaign' Committee because they felt this was simply a camouflage for Council inaction over its own internal racist policies and practices.

The appointment of a new Chairman to the Committee, Cllr Paul Lafferty with no prior experience whatsoever of race issues (though Cllr Hood remained as his Deputy), provided yet further cause for concern that the Race Relations Liaison Committee was simply a token structure belying a fundamental lack of interest and hostility from the core Labour leadership. As a result of this well-publicised pressure from the Caucus for some statement of Council commitment, a very brief District Labour Party statement was eventually produced announcing commitment to the work of the Race Relations Liaison Committee and expressing some support for limited monitoring and a vague acceptance of the necessity for some kind of positive action to counter discrimination. The Caucus argued that this needed to be strengthened, made more explicit and much more detailed but whilst the scope of this policy statement was still being debated the Labour leadership came forward with a practical proposal to actually implement the Central Race Relations Unit in the very near future.

The Caucus were pleased with what, on the surface, appeared to be a significant success in finally winning a practical agreement to implement the initiative that had been argued for since the campaign for the Equal Opportunity Policy in 1980. It seemed that their tough negotiating stance had paid off at last. Thus the Council accepted the need for a Race Relations Unit, established in the Chief Executive's Office, headed by a Principal Race Relations Adviser, with two appointments of Social Services and Personnel Advisers being finally made to complement the existing Housing and Education Advisers; there would be a Race Training Officer, a Research Officer, a Complaints Officer, and a Clerical Officer. It was accepted that two members of the Caucus would be involved in the short-listing and appointment procedure with full voting rights (the number was later extended to three), and though the Caucus tried to make some changes in the status of some of the posts which they argued should have been at a more senior level to give them more influence within the Council structure, by and large the proposal was broadly acceptable to the Caucus (it contained many of the Caucus' long canvassed demands), who therefore agreed that the appointment process should begin.

Little did the Caucus realise, at the time, that the Unit was being planned by Labour's Militant leadership not as a mechanism to ensure the implementation of racial equality policies and greater black access to the decision-making process, but as a means for Militant and its allies to assert its total control and power over the black community whose public opposition to aspects of Labour policy and practice was becoming a source of embarrassment and anger to the Labour leadership, and an independent political challenge that they had decided to find ways to suppress.

LIVERPOOL
City Council

SOLICITOR AND SECRETARY'S DEPARTMENT

In furtherance of the Council's Equal Opportunity Policy, a central Race Relations Unit has been established and applications are now invited for the following posts:

PRINCIPAL RACE RELATIONS ADVISER
(14,379-£15,357)
(Pay award pending)

To be responsible to the Chief Executive for the co-ordination and direction of the activities of the race relations advisers to ensure that the corporate approach on matters of race relations conforms to the Council's Equal Opportunity Policy. In this regard, the post holder will be expected to encourage initiatives in the fields of employment and service provision.

RACE RELATIONS ADVISER (SOCIAL SERVICES)
(£10,242-£11,052)
(Pay award pending)

To seek to improve the relevance of the services provided to the black communities by, principally, the Social Services Department. To achieve this, the post holder will spend much of his/her time seconded to the Social Services Department.

RACE RELATIONS ADVISER (EMPLOYMENT)
(£10,242-£11,052)
(Pay award pending)

The post holder will be seconded to the Central Personnel Unit and will examine all aspects of employment policy and practice to ensure the effective application of the Equal Opportunity Policy. This will include the investigation of monitoring arrangements and the preparation of reports and liaison with appropriate senior officers in connection with any proposals formulated.

The successful candidates should possess either a professional qualification, recognised in Local Government, or a relevant academic qualification. Evidence of work (voluntary or otherwise) with ethnic minorities is essential.

RACE RESEARCH OFFICER
(£9.060-£9,660)
(Pay award pending)

To undertake programmes of research into the provision of services to ethnic minorities. This will involve the evaluation and presentation of statistical data.

RACE TRAINING OFFICER
(£8,154-£8,712)
(Pay award pending)

To assist in the development of training programmes for employees of the Authority designed to cultivate an awareness of race relations issues in the provision of services and in employment

RACE COMPLAINTS OFFICER
(£8,154-£8,712)
(Pay award pending)

To assist with investigations and casework as appropriate in respect of complaints lodged in connection with service provision that appear to have or may have racial aspects.

ADMINISTRATIVE ASSISTANT
(£5,640-£6,135)
(Pay award pending)

To provide administrative and clerical support to the officers of the Central Race Relations Unit.

The successful candidates should possess appropriate professional or academic qualifications.

General Local Government Conditions of Service apply and removal expenses, to a maximum of £1,250 and temporary lodging allowance will be paid in appropriate cases.

APPLICATION FORMS, RETURNABLE BY 20 AUGUST 1984, TOGETHER WITH FURTHER DETAILS MAY BE OBTAINED FROM THE DIRECTOR OF PERSONNEL AND MANAGEMENT SERVICES, P.O. BOX 88, MUNICIPAL BUILDINGS, DALE STREET, LIVERPOOL L69 2DH (051-227 3911 EXT 705).

The City Council is an Equal Opportunity Employer and welcomes applications irrespective of race, sex, marital status or disability.

FROM THE OFFICE OF THE LEADER OF THE CITY COUNCIL
P.O.BOX 88
MUNICIPAL BUILDINGS,
LIVERPOOL, L69 2DH.

Telephone: 051- 227 3911 Ext.

FINAL

1³ After consultation with Black Organisations we beleive that the appointment yesterday ~~of Sam Bond~~ ~~was Made in error and~~ contary to the advice of Black Caucus Members who were present at the interview³

1   We want the reversal of the appointment of the Principal Advisor with the provision the post of Principal Race Relations Officer be re-advertised Previous applicants be invited to apply. ~~with the exception of person who are lacking in the experience of Liverpool Black issues³~~

2³ We want all posts being re-advertsided an appointmentsbeing made within the given time³

3³ We want the Labour Party to speak publicly about their support for the Unit³

4³ We want no victimisation of people involved in this action³

+ Further discussion will be held on the composition of the Examining Panel + the R.R cttee and the type of people needed for the jobs in in the race Relation Unit

4   The Sampson Bond Affair:
The Disputed Principal Race Relations Adviser Appointment

We have seen then that prior to the interviews for the post of Principal Race Relations Adviser and for the other planned posts in the Race Relations Unit, there had been fairly sharp disagreements at times between the Caucus and the Council, including a well-publicised walk-out from one meeting and ongoing criticism from the Caucus over the lack of Council action on many fronts, such as filling various agreed Section 11 posts, support for the positive action training scheme, or proposals for ethnic monitoring in the housing field; and there had been bitter conflict over the Council's last-minute abandonment of the River Avon Street sheltered housing scheme.

But the agreement of the Council to set up the Race Relations Unit, seen by the Caucus as one of the most significant of the demands they had been making, signalled the possibility of a new era in the implementation of the Council's Equal Opportunity Policy, and a major concession by the Labour leadership that perhaps promised a new partnership between the Labour Party and the black community.

The following eye-witness account by a member of the Caucus who was on the interviewing committee for the Principal Adviser post indicates the expectations of the Caucus members that there would be a fair series of interviews, out of which would emerge a strong Race Relations Unit that would, at last, open the way to some serious initiatives to promote racial equality policies and practices in Liverpool. In hindsight, of course, this indicated the political naivety of the Caucus, but at this time the issues of political appointments, attacks on voluntary groups and abuse of power later levelled at the Labour Group, were not yet the matters of regular public exposure that they have since become.

We now know that far from being a valuable catalyst for change, the appointment in fact led to the total break-down of relationships between the Council and the local black community, and to the abandonment of the City's Equal Opportunity Policy as well as to the abolition of the City's Race Relations Liaison Committee. It is therefore important for an understanding of what followed, to look very carefully at the actual appointment itself. We therefore reproduce in full the eye-witness accounts of the whole appointment process that were submitted to the National Executive Committee of the Labour Party in their investigation into malpractices in the Liverpool Labour Party.

It is important to stress that the Caucus representatives were present on the interviewing panel as fully legitimate, voting members of the Race Relations Liaison Committee which was itself accepted by all three parties as the authentic "representative" body advising the Council on race issues. This has to be emphasised, as immediately *after* the appointment was made, the Labour Party's principal attack was that the Caucus was an "unrepresentative and self-interested clique", with the *official* position of the Caucus within the City Council and on the appointments committee suddenly obliterated.

EYE WITNESS ACCOUNTS OF THE PRINCIPAL RACE RELATIONS ADVISER APPOINTMENT

(i) BLACK CAUCUS REPRESENTATIVE

(a) *Shortlisting Meeting* (Monday October 1st 1984)
I attended the short-listing meeting together with two colleagues as representatives of the Black Caucus on the appointments panel of the post in the Race Relations Unit.

Prior to the meeting, we had been sent summary sheets of each of the candidate's qualifications and experience — it had been agreed that we would be present as full voting members of the appointments sub-committee. In the first instance, two representatives were agreed but an extension to three voting members was accepted.

The meeting was also attended by Councillor Derek Hatton (in the chair), Councillor Paul Lafferty (Chair Race Relations Liaison Committee), Councillor Tony Hood (Vice Chair Race Relations Committee); Director of Personnel, a Social Services Department representative, a NALGO member and a few other officials.

The task of the meeting was to produce short-lists for a large number of posts in the Unit, (Principal, Social Services Adviser, Personnel Adviser, Training Officer, Research Officer, Complaints Officer and Clerical Officer). I assumed this would take the whole afternoon, but Councillor Hatton said he had to leave at 3.00 p.m. and planned to sort it all out by then. We expressed our doubts that it would be done as quickly as that.

There was some brief preliminary discussion — over voting rights, establishing that the three of us now had full rights on the committee; on procedure of interviews, with our suggestion being agreed that the principal Adviser be appointed first, and then would be able to sit-in on the selection of the rest of the Unit; on criteria for the appointment, when we said that we would be looking for people with the appropriate qualifications and experience: at which point Councillor Hatton said they would also be looking for someone to carry out Council policy.

A similar procedure was carried out for each of the posts — Councillor Hatton read out his prepared short-list and invited us to make comments and other nominations. Throughout the discussion, he accepted all of our own particular nominations and on some of his original list, was prepared to drop one or two names — thus the overall atmosphere appeared on the surface to be a reasonable spirit of give and take.

However, there were several abnormalities within this pattern which, of course in hindsight, prepared the way for what was to emerge at a later date.

With respect to the Principal Adviser, the one name Councillor Hatton insisted on retaining was that of Mr Sampson Bond, a London building surveyor, who had not been on my own personal proposed short list nor, as it transpired, on that of either of my two colleagues.

From the 'summary sheets' that had been sent out to us, there was absolutely no indication whatsoever that Mr Bond had any basis for applying for this post. He was not working professionally in the field of race relations and had never done so; his only job had been as a building surveyor which was his professional qualification; he referred only very vaguely to working to combat racism with black organisations; he was only aged 26, itself problematic for a senior officer to head a unit of 9 staff (the 7 to be appointed plus two already in post, Education and Housing Advisers).

We argued strongly that we could see no reason for his inclusion in the list; Councillor Hatton said he had seen the full letter of application, which he was not prepared at that time to let us examine, and this fuller form demonstrated Mr Bond's credentials to be short-listed. After all, he argued, he had not opposed any of the individual nominations put forward by us, he had removed other names at our request (perhaps the nominations put in by the Chief Officer concerned) and as Chair of the Committee he was going to insist that this name stays in.

In hindsight, that was perhaps the point at which we should have disassociated ourselves from the whole procedure and tried to prevent any further progress — but I'm afraid that we were obviously lulled into a position of trust in the appointment procedure due to the general atmosphere of compromise and the normal acceptance of our proposals. It should be noted that throughout the proceedings, no-one took any meaningful part in the discussions except Councillor Hatton and the three of us, with an occasional comment by the Personnel Director, when requested to do so by the Chair.

On the other posts, the major abnormality was in the short-listing for the post of Training Officer, when once again Councillor Hatton insisted on keeping from his original list a candidate with absolutely no apparent qualification. In hindsight, it seems possible that Councillor Hatton would have tried to secure his appointment as Race Relations Training Officer, despite his total lack of experience in this field.

It is also possible that there were other hand-picked candidates, which at the time were not so obvious — thus in employment, for which the field was not very strong, in hindsight, Councillor Hatton's nomination of Mr Kevin Fernandes from London, a British Rail clerical officer whose application bears similarities to Mr Bond's in terms of vague references to being "involved in black groups and campaigns", was probably the precursor of another pre-determined decision. Thus Mr Fernandes' name appears in *Militant* as a journalist/correspondent on 1st November, 1985.

The only other item of any possible significance was the absence both of the Chief Executive in whose department the unit was to be placed and the Community Liaison Officer with long experience of working with Black groups in the City. We specifically asked, at the end of the meeting that the Community Liaison Officer took part in the final interview — this was agreed, but, in fact, he was not included again in that forum, when only the Chief Executive and the Director of Personnel were present.

The interviews were to be held on Tuesday, 9th October, Wednesday, 10th October and Friday, 12th October. Only the interviews for the Race Adviser (Principal Officer) were held in full — for the Social Services post only 1 candidate in fact was interviewed, because, by then, the news of the walk-out by the black representatives and the union had begun to spread. By the next morning, the NALGO and Black community picket prevented any further interviews from taking place.

(b) *Interview Principal Race Adviser* (Tuesday, 9th October, 1984)
The interview panel consisted of 6 Labour Councillors (Cllrs Hatton, Lucock, Lafferty, Ord, Hood and Dillon); one Liberal Councillor (Cllr Pam Bradley); (apologies from the Conservative Councillor who was at the Conservative Party Congress); the three of us representing the Black Caucus; NALGO observer; Chief Executive, Director of Personnel and one or two minor officials.

At the beginning of the meeting, Cllr Hatton outlined the procedure, which consisted of him asking a number of standard questions, the rest of us to ask just one question each of our choice (but to try not to repeat others' questions, to save time) — the candidates would be interviewed first, then we would have lunch and discuss all applicants together after lunch.

He also stated that (direct quotes are taken from notes written during the interviews) "we are looking for someone supporting the policies of the Labour Party" — they would have to show "commitment to the policies we have been arguing for". At this point I immediately stated that we would be looking for someone with experience of negotiating and developing Equal Opportunity Policies, which required a considerable track-record in working with the local authority, councillors, officials and trade unions and in working with black groups; I also stressed that it was essential for the person to display a very good understanding of the particular race problems within Liverpool. My two colleagues supported those points, but there was no further debate on this issue.

The candidates were then interviewed, one at a time, in a fairly standard way. Each candidate was first of all asked some or all of the following questions by Councillor Hatton:

(i) Have you anything to add to your application?
(ii) What are your views on positive discrimination?
(iii) What are your views on ethnic monitoring?
(iv) What are the causes of discrimination?
(v) What is the role of the trade unions in this field?
(vi) What do you think of the problem of the white back-lash?

There was some difference in the degree of questioning and the types of issues put to the other candidates — but to me there was an overwhelming difference in the quality and nature of the responses given by Mr Bond as compared to the rest of the candidates.

On 'positive discrimination', each candidate, other than Mr Bond, made it clear that under existing legislation, positive discrimination is normally unlawful but that there is considerable scope for 'positive action' initiatives which are essential to any meaningful equal opportunity policy. Mr Bond, however, said positive discrimination does not solve problems, it was dangerous, led to greater divisions etc. He significantly said nothing about the need for 'positive action'.

On 'ethnic monitoring', each candidate other than Mr Bond said that monitoring was an essential tool with which to implement a serious equal opportunity policy, though adequate safeguards and support from black groups and trade unions had to be built in. Mr Bond, however, said that he was not in favour of monitoring and offered no comment on its potential value.

On the cause of discrimination, the candidates other than Mr Bond talked about the way racism was institutionalised in policies and practices of organisations and therefore had to be removed by practical measures to change policies and practices in an anti-racist direction; Mr Bond said that it was a question of urban deprivation and the Government's divide and rule policy and could only be tackled by the policy such as that of the Labour Council in Liverpool in taking on the government and building more houses and protecting and creating jobs.

On these particular set questions, Mr Bond's answers were quite confident and firm though delivered as if it was a prepared speech given to questions he already knew were going to be asked.

However, after this initial set, a most extraordinary sequence of events took place: Cllr Lucock asked him a question he had put to several other candidates about their experience and ideas about management — this in the context of a post which would involve being the head of a Unit which itself consisted of fairly senior advisers working in all major areas of the Authority's service provision. At this point, Mr Bond literally could not answer the question — Cllr Lucock repeated it, two other Labour Councillors also came in to ask the same question in a slightly different way, and again he just sat silently throughout, clearly in our view being totally unable to answer the question. Cllr Bradley the Liberal Councillor also raised this point and it became quite evident that Mr Bond had not had any management experience before and had not given any thought whatsoever to this important part of the work — at the end of this discussion, all he could say were some disparaging remarks about other race units providing too much paper and reports with Advisers drawing good salaries, and being out of touch with the "grass-roots" — he would "consult and liaise with the community".

From this point, Mr Bond's answers were vague and over-general and in my view indicated a total lack of awareness of, or commitment to, the specific measures required to be developed by the Race Unit to promote equal opportunities in the field of race relations. It was clear he had no relevant experience or qualifications for the post, in terms of his own practical training, his work experience, or his voluntary record of relevant work.

I myself quizzed him with some intensity to find out what exactly his experience had been in the field: after a number of very vague answers he said he had been involved in the 'Sus Campaign' and also 'New Cross Massacres Campaign' — but it was clear that he had held no position of responsibility or authority in either of these campaigns, both of which had, in any case, little to do with public sector equal opportunity policy-making. He made general reference to 'Youth Work' but again provided no specific answers to what formal positions he had held. Again, in answer to his experience of race training, it transpired that he had simply attended a training session as a council employee, along with other employees in Brent. He 'dropped' Cllr. Russell Profitt's name in this context, Brent's Race Adviser — (but Profitt has, since, publicly said that he had no previous knowledge of Bond whatsoever.)

December 13, 1984

Sam Bond—a city's 'recipe for disaster'

by David Heal

A RACE RELATIONS expert yesterday warned Liverpool City Council they were cooking up a "recipe for disaster" with the Sam Bond job controversy.

Russell Profitt, race relations adviser for Brent Council in London, where Mr Bond worked until his arrival in Liverpool this week, said the appointment was an "offence to the black community in the city."

Mr Profitt, deputy leader of Lewisham Council, and a former prospective Labour Parliamentary candidate, added that Mr Bond's position as a £14,000 a year race relations adviser would do an embarrassment to the Labour Party.

And Mr Profitt said: "I would not have short-listed Mr Bond for a race relations job in Liverpool, Lewisham or in Brent. The issue here is his lack of experience. It is an extraordinarily complex job.

"His name is not well-known within Brent com-

Russell Profitt   *Sam Bond*

munities for work on the race issue, or in and around London. I think he made a contribution once to a seminar on the question of race.

"I think the Liverpool City Council and the local Labour Party have created for themselves a crisis born out of their lack of trust in the black community. Their approach is totally insulting and must change."

Mr Profitt was speaking at

Liverpool University yesterday at a conference, "Racial Equality in Employment on Merseyside", where he talked of the "London experience".

Brent has the largest race unit in any of the London boroughs, working to promote positive action on race matters, yet Mr Bond was not known to the unit as a worker on the race issue.

"Liverpool City Council is refusing to face up to the

need to take positive action on race relations, particularly in recruitment.

"The race relations adviser must have strong links with the black community and this isn't the case in Liverpool, nor is it likely to be if the city continues with the appointment of Mr Bond, and refuses discussions with the leaders of the black caucus to establish what demands the black community has.

"I don't know for a fact that Mr Bond belongs to any particular political group, but it's news to me if he has, as it says in his recent press statement, "campaigned for anti-racist policies".

Another speaker at the conference yesterday was Mr Peter Newsam, chairman of the Commission for Racial Equality, who said the CRE had been assured formally by Liverpool City Council that Mr Bond's appointment was made in accordance with the law on race relations.

"We are obviously concerned about problems in relation to this issue, but we

cannot stand between elected representatives and the electorate.

"But we will be watching any relationships that follow this appointment, and will do anything we can to help."

Earlier, Mr Alex Bennett, senior community officer for the Merseyside Community Relations Council, and an opponent of the Bond appointment, said the black community in Liverpool had not improved their housing, employment or social conditions since the Toxteth riots, and he accused city politicians and employers of being "skilled racists" by not giving more jobs to the non-white community.

No city councillors who were invited to yesterday's prestigious conference attended. Merseyside County Council leader Keva Coombes opened the day's proceedings.

News advertisements appeared yesterday for a Race Relations Officer for Merseyside County Council on a salary between £11,703 and £12,738.

Again, when my colleagues asked him about race issues in Liverpool, all he could say was that black people's problems were the same all over the country, there was not anything different about Liverpool — he showed no awareness of different minorities in the city, their particular histories etc., particularly the unique nature of the Liverpool born Black community.

It was quite clear in my own mind that Bond was totally unqualified and unsuitable for this post — in this context he was in a category quite on his own, with the other 5 candidates each having a wealth of experience and knowledge of equal opportunity policy compared to Mr Bond, and each demonstrating a commitment to practical policy changes in this field as well as experience and ideas concerning management and leadership. (The other candidates were all involved in full-time race relations work, whether as local authority advisers, in the voluntary sector or in research, and all had excellent track-records in working with black organisations).

After lunch, Cllr Hatton began — he stated that the major issue to him was appointing someone who would carry out Council policies as put forward by the Labour Party. On this basis, he ruled out two local candidates whose attitudes to positive action, monitoring and Council policy were "out of line with Labour Party policies". Their involvement with the CRC and the Black Caucus showed that they could not carry out the functions of the Race Unit, because of the conflicts that had arisen over race policies with the Council and the Labour Party. Their loyalty was therefore questionable. Before ruling these two out, he had immediately excluded two further candidates (one local and one external), without explanation. The remaining local candidate was more suited to the Social Services Adviser post: that left Sam Bond, an excellent candidate who supported Labour policy and who, therefore, was his choice for the post.

Cllr Hatton then went around the room, first to the other 5 Labour Councillors; to my utter astonishment, each of the other Councillors with no hesitation, and with no question of wanting to hear the view point of the representatives of the black organisations, stated their preference for Bond. A number of them repeated the point about the need to appoint someone who will be loyal to Labour Party policy and about the critical roles played by two local candidates over Council policy. One should stay where he is because "he is doing a good job there". Another was "lacking in managerial experience"; another was "light weight". They each said how impressed they were with Bond and they each said that he was their first choice.

Pam Bradley, the Liberal Councillor, said that she could not agree with this — she was not impressed with Bond at all, but she was impressed with many other candidates, particularly two of the locals, one in particular who had conducted an excellent interview.

Going around the circle, at this point it was my turn to speak, which I did at length, having taken a little while to adjust to the shock of seeing that we were in danger of a 'fixed' appointment being made. I dealt at length with Bond's unsuitability on every count — experience, qualifications, knowledge, commitment and performance during the interview itself. I expanded on the vastly more extensive experience every other candidate had, and their performances in the interviews. I suggested that they were unfair and inconsistent about the performances of two of the local candidates, who were either simply doing their jobs in criticising Council policy or representing a group who had selected them. I pointed out that they had not raised the issue of 'loyalty' etc with them. I pointed out that one of the locals apparently seen as a serious candidate for the Social Services post by Hatton, was a part of the Black Caucus too. I also said that *Council* policy was currently in *favour* of taking positive action and was already undertaking ethnic monitoring in employment, therefore I argued Cllr Hatton's interpretation of whether these two candidates were out of line with Council policy was open to debate — indeed it was Cllr Hatton's views and those of Mr Bond that were perhaps out of line with

City Council Policy — I also reminded him that a recent District Labour Party Policy Document on race relations had given support to positive action and to monitoring. I then argued that Mr Bond should *not* be appointed, that *all* of the other 5 candidates were far more appropriate; and of these, in my own view, one of the local candidates was the most appropriate in terms of relevant all round experience, skills and knowledge.

My two colleagues totally supported my statement over Bond — they confirmed that his appointment was utterly unacceptable and that he was not a serious candidate. They agreed with me that all the other candidates were far superior to Bond, but they each said that they would put one of the other local candidates as their first choice.

At this point the dialogue between Hatton and ourselves continued a little further, with the Chief Executive making his sole contribution of the day which was to hope it would all work out harmoniously in the end; the Personnel Director said nothing throughout. We stressed that Bond's appointment would be totally unacceptable and we urged the Councillors not to go down a road that would inevitably bring the Council into conflict with the black community.

Hatton brought the matter to a vote, long before a full discussion had really taken place — he proposed Bond, Cllr Bradley put an amendment to the vote by nominating a local candidate — this was taken first: 4 for, 6 against.

The motion to appoint Bond was then put: 6 in favour (the Labour Cllrs) 4 against (Cllr Bradley and the three of us). At this point the three of us spontaneously stood up, said the appointment was totally unacceptable and walked out of the meeting as did the NALGO observer.

There can be no doubt that this appointment was 'fixed' in advance — the unanimity, lack of doubt amongst the Labour members in the face of a weak candidate facing competition from well qualified and capable people (including a Principal Race Adviser with a Labour-controlled Authority) is sure evidence for me that they had made up their minds in advance of the interviews. The rote delivery by Bond of his answers to the set questions indicate that he may very well have been briefed in advance himself on those questions and the expected answers. Hatton himself openly admitted that they were elevating "loyalty to Labour Policy" above any other criteria — whilst his stated interpretation of that policy, on 'positive action' and 'monitoring', is *in fact* out of line with *national Labour Party Policy*, with the *City Council's* explicit policy and arguably even with *District Labour Party* policy.

It is clear that a number of the Liverpool candidates were being discriminated against, without being given the opportunity in the interview situation of answering claims that they were opposed to the Council's Equal Opportunity Policy or that they might act improperly if they became Council employees because of their association with Merseyside Community Relations Council or the Black Caucus or the City's Race Relations Liaison Committee.

This view of the unfairness of the appointment process for the post of Principal Race Relations Adviser was held not just by the three Caucus representatives, as shown in the above statement; the official observer for NALGO was equally convinced that the appointment had involved discrimination against unsuccessful candidates.

EYE-WITNESS ACCOUNT — (ii) TRADE UNION (NALGO) OBSERVER

On the 9th October 1984, appointments were being held at the Municipal Buildings, Dale Street, for the Principal Race Relations Adviser. Grade PO6.

As a Nalgo representative, my duties were to ensure that the interviews were free from any form of discrimination.

There were six candidates for the above post, four of whom were from Liverpool and who had the necessary experience of the Liverpool black community and its inherent problems. They all had good experience in organising projects, liaison with the City Council and had a good knowledge of Labour Party Policy.

Although the fifth candidate was not from Merseyside, he is a Principal Race Adviser with valuable experience.

The final candidate, Mr Bond, is a Londoner and has been employed for two years as an Assistant Building Surveyor. He has spent two years in University for his building surveyors' posts. His experience consists of part-time youth work. Mr Bond gave a poor interview and had difficulty in understanding questions from the panel.

I felt that there was discrimination in that the other candidates were more experienced and projected themselves far better at their interviews.

Derek Hatton stated clearly that he was looking for someone to "toe the party line". This caused concern to the Caucus and Liberal Councillor as well as myself. They all stated that they were looking for someone with knowledge and experience of racial problems.

After the interviews took place, discussions were held between the Councillors and the Black Caucus on the above post.

Derek Hatton was the first Councillor to appoint Mr Bond. Derek Hatton said, "There were candidates who would have difficulty in following party policy because they have criticised policy in the past".

This caused great concern to myself and the Black Caucus and the Liberal Councillor. The Caucus said that it was the candidates' jobs to tell any political party where and how they are going wrong in Race Relations.

Derek Hatton then said to the Caucus they would be allowed to say what they felt when it was their turn. Derek Hatton then went on to say he felt Mr Bond was "New blood" and felt Mr Bond was a "Breath of fresh air".

A Councillor from the Labour Party chose to discriminate. He said "Candidates are doing a good job where they are, they can easily stay there, I go for Mr Bond".

Again concern was shown by the Caucus and they again said knowledge and experience was important and not someone to toe the party line.

The Caucus members, after pleading with the Councillors to listen to them, then stood up and felt they could not take part in the appointment of a young inexperienced candidate, whilst the other candidates portrayed a wealth of experience and knowledge.

In view of the performance of the other applicants, I felt that Mr Bond was not the best candidate for the job, after reading about his experience and watching his performance at the interview, I could no longer take part as a trade unionist, therefore I walked out and said I would have to report back to Nalgo on what I had seen and heard.

This view of the interview was upheld immediately by the local NALGO officials, on the grounds of "blatant political discrimination and irregularities" (*NALGO Herald* Vol. 2, No. 9, July, 1985).

The following statements by two members of the Labour Party that were passed onto the National Executive's Inquiry confirm quite irrefutably the certainty felt by the Black Caucus representatives as well as the NALGO observer that the appointment had been "fixed" in advance.

STATEMENT 1

On Tuesday, September 18th, 1984, I received a telephone call from Councillor Derek Hatton during which he listed the names of the people whom he intended to shortlist for the post of Race Relations Adviser, and he asked me what I knew about them.

The same Sam Bond was not mentioned on this shortlist.

After a discussion about the people shortlisted, Councillor Hatton informed me that he was going to London the next day to interview a 'Comrade' for the post of Race Relations Adviser.

The only name which appeared on the shortlist of names for this post other than those given to me by Councillor Hatton was that of Sam Bond.

STATEMENT 2

I declare that the following is a true but not verbatim account part of a conversation I had with Liverpool City Councillor Tony Byrne on the morning of January 7th, 1985.

I had noted that earlier in the conversation, Mr Byrne had said he had once advised a black family against moving their home to the North side of the city because of rampant racism. I said that I considered the black people of Liverpool to be as oppressed as any group within the country. He said that it was no more so than for poor whites. I reminded him of his comment earlier and pointed out that black people in Liverpool were kept in the ghetto that bordered by Park Road (because of white gangs), Kensington (because of the activities of the National Front) and the Bridge on Smithdown Road. I mentioned the recent report of the Community Relations Council on racial discrimination in council housing and asked what was being done about it.

In response, Mr Byrne said he did not believe in positive action, ie as he saw it, noting the ethnic origins of tenants. I said the black community were powerless to improve their condition, and that the purpose of erecting the post of Principal Race Relations Officer was precisely to give them a voice in the corridors of power, someone totally independent of the City Council, and able to confront the Council or any other responsible body. Sam Bond, I said, would not do that because he was in sympathy with Council thinking against that of the black community.

Mr Byrne told me that the Labour Party in Liverpool had its policy against racism but it was part of an overall battle against capitalist structures. Politics, he said, is about power. I entered politics to gain and to exercise power. We would be betraying what we stand for if we did not use power to the full. If that means that we must appoint those who agree with Council policy, then we will appoint them. We cannot afford to be distracted from our purpose. I said — even if it means that the black community are without their rightful representation? Mr Byrne said that as the party in power, with support of the electorate, the present Labour Council had to carry out its policy and it would.

He then went on to say that it was precisely to implement this policy that Sam Bond had been appointed. I then sought to clarify this and asked was everything planned beforehand. Mr Byrne said of course it was. He implied I was naive if I thought anything else. He said the Council had the power to implement its policy and it would have abused its responsibility and misused its power if it had not seen exactly where it was going.

Mr Byrne left me in no doubt that the appointment of Sam Bond was cut and dried before ever the interviews for the post took place.

TRADE UNION AND COMMUNITY PICKET AND SIT-IN IN COUNCILLOR HATTON'S OFFICE

The morning after the appointment of Mr Bond had taken place, an official NALGO picket was mounted at the Council buildings where the interviews for the rest of the posts in the Race Relations Unit were to have taken place. Members of a range of local black groups were present due to a word of mouth mobilisation that had taken place to support the walk-out by Black Caucus members of the previous day's interviews. The City Councillors, led by Councillor Hatton, who said that he would "take no notice of the Black Caucus picket", did not in fact go into the building because of the presence of the official NALGO picket and retreated to Councillor Hatton's office.

A delegation from the picket went to the office to urge the Labour Group to alter the course they had taken, as this would bring them into massive conflict with the local black community. The Councillors said they had made the appointment, and that was the end of the matter. When this was relayed back to the representatives picketing the municipal annexe, a group of about thirty people proceeded to Councillor Hatton's office and announced that they were sitting-in so that negotiations over the appointment could take place.

This sit-in has since become a matter of enormous controversy, and has been used by the Labour Group to denounce the Black Caucus in the most extreme terms. The Labour Group on the Liverpool City Council has always identified itself with militant Labour movement actions. It gave total support to the picketing miners, and consistently refused to denounce any of its more "violent" manifestations; it had recently given full support to the prolonged sit-in by the Cammell Laird workers protesting against redundancies; when in opposition, they had frequently been involved in the disruption of Council meetings or the public barracking of Conservative Government representatives. Its response to the sit-in by a predominantly black group of local people should be seen in that kind of broader political context.

The sit-in, as the Caucus have continually stressed, was entirely *peaceful*. A number of journalists wandered in and out of the offices. The Council's security force were present throughout the occupation. The police came at one point and were sent off by the Councillors as being unnecessary. In fact, Derek Hatton actually left the room with the police and then returned. At the end of the afternoon, after prolonged negotiations between Councillor Hatton and Black Caucus representatives, Councillor Hatton signed a document which agreed to re-advertise the post of Principal Race Relations Adviser. Councillor Hatton also appeared on the media and publicly stated that he had *not* been "forced" to sign the statement (see *Guardian* 11 October 1985 — "I was not threatened" — by Derek Hatton).

Statement signed by Derek Hatton

From the Office of the Leader of the City Council, 10th October, 1984.

1. After consultation with Black organisations we believe that the appointment yesterday was made contrary to the advice of Black Caucus Members who were present at the interview.
2. We want the reversal of the appointment of the Principal Advisor with the provision that the post of Principal Race Relations Officer be re-advertised, previous applicants be invited to apply and further discussions will be held on the composition of the interviewing panel and the Race Relations Committee and on the type of people needed for the jobs in the Race Relations Unit.

3. We want all posts to be re-advertised and appointments to be made within a given time.
4. We want the Labour Party to speak publicly about their support for the Unit.
5. We want no victimisation of people involved in this action.

Black 'siege' blocks race job

By Alan Dunn

The deputy leader of Liverpool City council dropped a controversial race relations appointment yesterday after being held in his office for more than five hours by 30 black activists.

Mr Derek Hatton agreed to have the post of principal race relations officer re-advertised, with previous applicants invited to re-apply. "It was not a case of giving in to the mob," he said. "I was not threatened. There were a lot of people there and we had to take notice of their strong feelings."

The confrontation followed the appointment on Tuesday of Mr Sampson Bond, an assistant building surveyor at Brent Council, in north London, to become the £14,000-a-year head of a new race relations unit.

Members of the Black Cau-cus, who advised the council on black affairs, walked out of the meeting of the personnel committee, complaining that Mr Bond lacked the necessary experience, qualifications and local knowledge to carry out "this responsible and sensitive position." There had been four local people in the shortlist of six.

Representatives of the black community saw Mr Hatton in his office at the municipal buildings yesterday and were later joined by more than 30 of their colleagues.

An agreed statement was withdrawn because it stated: "We still believe that Sam Bond is the best person for the job." A second statement omitted the words and the councillors left the building.

"We still believe that the decision was right but we had to defuse the situation and

Mr Derek Hatton — 'I was not threatened'

come to a reasonable conclusion," said Mr Hatton. "We refused to involve the police, preferring to continue our discussions."

Councillor Tony Mulhearn, president of the district Labour party, said: "Workers, black and white, support our

stand to develop harmonious race relations in the City.

A spokesman for the black community said that the action had been taken after talks within the community. She denied that councillors had been held against their will but had stayed because they were involved in a "big negotiation."

It had been agreed, she said, that the appointment had been made contrary to the advice of the Black Caucus members at the interview.

Should Mr Bond again be re-appointed it would "show that the Labour Party treats the black community with total disregard." Similar action could be taken again, she felt, because "we need strong people to guide the new unit which we regard as vital to the future of good race relations in the city."

Guardian, 11 October 1985

THE DISTRICT LABOUR PARTY MEETING

The agreement to readvertise the post was, however, short-lived, and the following evening a meeting of the District Labour Party took place which was crucially important in setting the tone of the local Labour Party's subsequent official view of the appointment, the sit-in, and the local black community. National controversy has raged over the role of Militant within the Labour Party in Liverpool and the alleged constitutional malpractices involving the District Labour Party composition and procedures, after Neil Kinnock's attack on Militant at the 1985 National Labour Party Conference. The fateful District Labour Party meeting on the evening of Thursday, 11th October, highlights some of the broader problems.

On that evening, a very strict control of the door was maintained by District Labour Party Secretary, Militant supporter Cllr Felicity Dowling. The status of members of District Labour Party meetings has been one of the reasons for the National Executive's shutting down of the District Labour Party, with 'aggregates' of members of the Labour Party (but not necessarily members of the District Committee) conducting Party business. On this particular meeting, however, the officials at the door were refusing entry to anyone whom they said were not full delegates to the District Party, though normal practice was to allow in 'observers' to meetings even if technically they could not vote. The political balance of the District Party at this time was one in which there was a clear majority for the Militant dominated leadership of the Council: a few trade union branches, sympathetic to Militant, controlled the majority of votes.

The 'delegates only' ruling meant that two Labour Party members of the Black Caucus were not allowed into the meeting, neither were two other black Labour Party members (there were hardly any black delegates to the District Party). The whole of the proceedings of the evening were devoted to a discussion of the appointment and of the sit-in. A proposal was put from the floor that the Caucus members should be allowed in to the meeting, to put forward their point of view, rather than being attacked in their absence, but this request was refused (a point to be borne in mind when reflecting on claims of Militant members that they were treated unfairly by Labour's National Executive). People who were present at the meeting were shocked at the way leading members of the Labour Group inflamed racist feelings amongst the membership by continuously stressing that they had been subjected to violence and abuse from the Black Caucus. The language of the resolution that was put, and carried by a large majority, expresses some of the racist assumptions and images that were conjured up by the various speakers for the motion: the occupiers used "intimidation and threats", held councillors "hostage", a method "*allien* (sic) to the Labour movement"; councillors signed under "duress", were held as "prisoners": all this by an "unrepresentative group" seeking to appoint "one of their own".

LIVERPOOL DISTRICT LABOUR PARTY RESOLUTION

The District Labour Party reaffirms its policy of implacably opposing division between black and white workers and it opposes discrimination against anyone on grounds of colour, sex or creed, in employment and services. We support the City Council in establishing a Race Relations Unit to assist in race relations and to combat incidents of racism.

However, the DLP condemns the use of intimidation and threats by those who occupied the office of the Council Leader and Deputy Leader. The councillors were held as hostages, completely against their will — a method alien to the Labour movement. The DLP recognises that the councillors only signed a statement under duress. Notwithstanding, the DLP endorses — and instructs the councillors to reaffirm — the appointment of Sampson Bond, who was properly interviewed and found to be the most able candidate as Principal Race Relations Advisor, by the interview panel. This Party refuses to allow any councillors, who were democratically elected by the people of Liverpool, to be held by ANY unrepresentative group whether black or white, who seek to impose their will on elected councillors.

The Council has a duty to represent the interests of the whole community, including all ethnic minorities, and cannot succumb to a small, unrepresentative group who only seek to have one of their own nominees appointed to the job.

Furthermore, in addition to damaging race relations in Liverpool, these actions involved holding councillors as prisoners, which completely diverted them from using the City Council meeting to support the fight of the Cammell Lairds Trade Unionists who are imprisoned by the Tories. We look forward to the immediate use of the Race Relations Unit to fight against racism and strengthen working class unity in Liverpool.

The Labour Party.

At this meeting then, war was officially declared by the leadership of the District Labour Party on the organised black community in Liverpool, with the slurs of "violence" and "unrepresentativeness" being the constant twin themes of the assault on the hitherto fully accepted and legitimate leading organisations working with local black and ethnic minority groups. On the Labour Party side, this struggle involved a massive propaganda effort using the resources of the *Militant* newspaper and the District Labour Party and Young Socialist machines, as well as official Council publications. It also involved the attempt to actively mobilise a group of 'imported' Militant full-timers to work with Sampson Bond in the Liverpool 8 area and to set up a Militant 'front' organisation (Merseyside Action Group) later assisted by a second contested political appointment; it also entered into a shadowy area connecting orthodox politics with less orthodox use of money and muscle-power, which has given rise to allegations of attempts by Militant to win support for themselves and their figure-head, Sampson Bond, through financial bribery and physical force. On the other side, the battle has involved a two year stand by the overwhelming majority of local black groups in boycotting the work of Sampson Bond, supported by most of the local authority trade unions, several constituency and ward Labour Parties, the Liberal Party, the Communist Party, the churches and much of the local voluntary sector. The outcome of this struggle certainly entailed for the first time serious public doubt over the activities of the Militant-led Labour Party, and serious division amongst the ranks of their supporters. It has, arguably, been one of the causes of the ultimate official demise of the Militant leadership of Merseyside. A close analysis of the way Militant waged this campaign, and the opposition that the Black Caucus was able to mobilise, should provide many clues to both the strength and the ultimate weakness of Merseyside's Militants: it will also help clarify the ways in which Militant and their supporters have clearly gone beyond the pale of acceptable methods of political organisation and activity, and how these malpractices have been frequently colluded in by non-Militant members of the Labour Party in Liverpool.

5 Militant's War on the Black Community: 1984-1986

We have seen how Militant and their supporters began their frontal attack on Liverpool's black community at the special District Labour Party by their concerted vilification of black community groups as "violent", "unrepresentative", "criminal" and "self-interested". Of course, this approach to dealing with the black community's active opposition to Labour's unjust appointment of Sampson Bond, by means of a series of slurs and stereotypes, was no different in kind to the attempts by the police, by sections of the 'popular' press, and by right-wing commentators to explain away the grievances felt by black people in Liverpool and elsewhere which underlay the 'riots' of 1981. The unscrupulous willingness of Labour's local leadership to use the repertoire of racist language and emotion in this way as part of their political project has been one of the most shameful aspects of this issue.

There seems no doubt that the leading group around Militant were deeply shaken by the response of organisations in the black community to refuse to go along with their 'fixed' appointment and to express this opposition in such a high-profile, public manner. To have been caught out and exposed in this humiliating way, and in an area as sensitive as the race relations field, clearly represented a major public challenge to Militant. Rather than attempting to resolve the problem in a constructive way, they chose instead to mount an all-out ideological offensive against the black community and their representatives together with a major organisational operation to try to divide the black community, and to win support amongst the Labour movement which was clearly at risk given NALGO's official boycott of the Bond appointment.

However, the black organisations and race relations agencies themselves were not passively spectating whilst Militant mobilised against them. They also realised the importance of building support within the black community, within the Labour movement and within the wider public over the question of the appointment and the broader issues of race policy and the legitimacy of the black representation on the city's Race Relations Liaison Committee raised by the publicity given to the appointment, the sit-in and the boycott.

A major struggle then was waged, certainly the most sustained opposition that Militant had faced since taking office, and one which entailed a major split within the Labour Party and a serious loss of public credibility for the Labour leadership. In retrospect, it seems an extraordinary decision by Labour's ruling inner circle to take the risk of embarking on this major struggle with the black community in Liverpool, but this short-sighted political approach, of being determined to crush all political opposition at whatever the cost and by whatever means necessary however damaging or disreputable (presumably under the old-fashioned Stalinist view that "the end always justifies the means") has been the hallmark of Militant's period of office. Ultimately this greed for control and total power, to be exercised by the inner circle of the ruling Party alone, or by their trusted and proven creatures, proved their undoing, together with their ultimately subjectivist approach to politics that made them refuse to move beyond the flights of rhetoric to a realistic calculation of the effects of their actions.

It is this continual use of all the classical features of Stalinist politics that stand out in analysing the approach adopted by Militant to the black community in Liverpool: the character asassination of opponents; the crushing of dissent; the voluntarist and rhetorical substitution of fantasy for reality in strategic thinking; the development of 'front' organisations as well as individual patronage in appointments; the concentration of enormous power in the hands of a few key individuals (Cllr Hatton, the public figure-head, Cllr Mulhearn, the party fixer, Mr Ian Lowes the trade union boss, and close 'non-Militant' ally Cllr Byrne the financial power behind the Council's day to day operations including its ambitious urban regeneration programme); the control and manipulation by various gerry-mandering devices of the Party machine whose meetings were increasingly described as Nuremberg rallies because of the intimidation, workerism and physical menace lying behind the classical calls for "unanimity" in the "working-class" struggle. Of course, other features of local socio-economic and political realities have also to be included in a total analysis of this period including the genuine problems facing Liverpool in terms of Government cuts, previous financial under-budgeting by the Liberal administrations, the historic weakness and oligarchic nature of the Labour Party in Liverpool which was prey to the Trotskyist entryism of Militant, the ideological predominance of workerism in the Labour movement in Liverpool as a whole and the absence of a strong, coherent and organised non-Militant left.

These then are some of the political traditions involved in the tactics followed by Militant in this struggle. In addition, the Labour Party enjoyed outright political control in the Council and the Labour Group accepted a version of "democratic centralism" which involved both accepting the District Labour Party as the source of all decisions to be taken by the Labour Group in Council and the unquestioning acceptance of all decisions taken by the representatives of the Labour Group, in whom, in fact, enormous decision-making powers were increasingly vested. This clear political control enabled the total power and resources of the local state to be concentrated in the hands of Militant and their supporters and fellow-travellers, which was again clearly illustrated during the course of this dispute. The relative weakness and compliance of senior council officials that we noted during the Bond appointment process is also important to consider, as is the general reluctance of the local trade union movement to publicly oppose or criticise the Council leadership (a taboo not really shaken until redundancies were delivered to City Council employees in autumn 1985).

Ranged on the other side of this struggle was the network of black organisations that had been involved in the Black Caucus, which included most of the agencies and groups active in the Liverpool 8 area and in the anti-racist struggle generally, plus, in the first instance, the trade union NALGO which had made the boycott of Bond's appointment official at the beginning of the dispute. A relatively small minority then was being forced to take on the might of the Militant machine, with their control over the District Labour Party and the Labour Movement together with access to and control over the resources of the local state. Although the black organisations had right on their side, the Militant Tendency must have thought theirs would be an easy victory. However, the forces proved to be very evenly matched, and by the end of the contest it was Militant's official empire that was finally undermined, whereas the black community's stand, which had contributed to the fall of Militant's Liverpool leadership, remained extraordinarily solid despite two years of intense pressure and struggle.

THE STRUGGLE FOR THE SUPPORT OF THE LABOUR MOVEMENT

The leadership of the Liverpool Labour Party during this period exerted much of its authority from its claims to represent the working-class movement. Indeed, much of the actual political position of the leading group derived from its direct control over the trade union block votes within the District Labour Party exercised through a few branches of the GMBATU and the TGWU. These "sweet-heart" union branches, as the local media has called them, have provided the basis of Militant's control, and an elaborate system of patronage developed which bound union members to Militant's inner sanctum through nomination rights exercised by a few unions, ultimate control over appointments enjoyed by Cllr Derek Hatton (Personnel Chairman) and votes in the District Labour Party exercised by these council workers, mediated through their leaders. In addition to the control of individual unions branches, a broader political control over the workforce was maintained by means of the Joint Shop Stewards Committee, originally led on a broader base by forces close to or in the Communist Party but increasingly during this period becoming a mainstay of support for Labour Party policies, though far less rigidly controlled than the District Labour Party thanks to the continued involvement of Communist Party members and independent left-wingers in the Committee.

It was vital, then, for Militant in terms of its general pretensions to working-class leadership to try to win support from the organised Labour movement for its appointment of Sampson Bond. The central focus for this struggle was clearly NALGO, as it was this union which had officially boycotted the appointment, and all subsequent appointments in the Race Relations Unit. NALGO took a very firm line on the dispute from the outset. Their observer maintained that political discrimination had taken place during the interviews, and the local NALGO executive confirmed this decision. NALGO (unlike the District Labour Party) allowed representatives from both the Labour Group as well as from the Black Caucus to put their case to union meetings and, after hearing all sides of the argument, NALGO members gave overwhelming backing to the boycott of all Race Unit posts, including Sampson Bond. This boycott was officially backed by NALGO's National Emergency Committee shortly afterwards and, indeed, at national level, Brent NALGO (Bond's own union branch) accepted the NEC decision.

This was a most significant set of decisions, constituting a major setback for Militant which they had tried to prevent by using a range of manoeuvres: they had written direct to all NALGO members, by-passing the official trade union (a tactic, according to NALGO "devised by Michael Edwardes and perfected by Ian MacGregor — strange bed-fellows for the Labour Group": *Nalgo Herald* Vol. 2, No. 9, July, 1985), with a mixture of "misinformation, lies and pomposity"; the Militant Leadership also conducted, again, a campaign of character-assassination against the leadership of NALGO, accusing them of being "treacherous" and a "bunch of Tories" in opposing Labour on this issue (*Merseyside Labour Briefing* Feb/March, 1985). Despite all these efforts at sabotage NALGO maintained the boycott throughout the two-year period, an indispensable ingredient in the success of the whole campaign. Within NALGO itself, the existence of an organised Black Workers' Group played an important role in ensuring that the Union maintained its position and local officers of NALGO took an uncompromising and consistent stance on this issue.

Race Relations Unit - Official Boycott

The General Secretary has written to all branches, advising them that all members are officially "authorised and strongly urged not to co-operate with any work arising out of the proposed Race Relations Unit", and that all the vacant posts in the Unit are officially boycotted. The background to the boycott has been widely publicised, and a radio report, which alleged that NALGO nationally was not supporting the Branch, was totally incorrect.

Accordingly, all members of NALGO are officially urged and authorised to not co-operate with any work arising from the Race Relations Unit, and are officially instructed not to carry out any work attached to the vacant, boycotted posts in the Unit. This official instruction includes the following work, which is included in the job descriptions for the boycotted posts:

1. Development and operation of training programmes;
2. Undertaking of research programmes;
3. Monitoring of complaints which have racial overtones;
4. Delivery of any monitoring information (concerning jobs or service delivery) to the Principal Adviser;
5. All administrative and clerical support to the unit, including typing, filing, photocopying, note-taking etc.;
6. Any further work which would be done by the boycotted posts.

When any member refuses to undertake work in connection with the above authorisation other members are instructed not to subsequently carry out that work.

COUNCIL BUDGET : BOND AFFAIR

NALGO WILL FIGHT ON BOUND FRONTS!

Pete Creswell
Secretary
Liverpool NALGO

Throughout the first half of 1984, Liverpool NALGO ran a campaign - "Our City- Our Fight" - which was virtually un paralleled in NALGO'S history. It was designed to gain support for the City Council's stand against Government cuts, and was the biggest campaign run by any union in the City. On every demonstration, NALGO's was the biggest sinle union contingent, and the strike on 29th March was almost 100% solid amongst NALGO members.

Now, a few months later, NALGO is being described(privately) by some Labour Councillors as "treacherous" and " a bunch of Tories" (sic). One Councillor has said that he expects NALGO to betray the Council during the next stage of the campaign.

NO BACKING DOWN

What is the reason for such a dramatic turnaround? OK, you guessed it - the "Sam Bond affair"! NALGO has had the unprecedented gall to actually stand up to the City Council, and has told the District Labour Party that no matter how much they stamp their feet, we have no intention of backing down.

The immediate cause of the dispute is the blatant discrimination which took place at the interview for the post of Principal Race Relatics Advisor. The NALGO representative at the interview reported that the Labour Councillors had appointed the least experienced, and least suitable candidate, purely on the grounds that his views coincided with those of the District Labour Party. But apart from anything else, the DLP policy on race is vague and

contradictory. In a consultative document issued in August 1984 the DLP states its support for positive action, monitoring,and a "fair reflection of the black population in the Council's workforce as soon as possible". Yet in defending Bond's appointment Derek Hatton has said that they could not appoint anyone who supported positive action, monitoring or targets! Paul Lucock, speaking at a NALGO meeting, went even further.

He said that certain candidates were not acceptable because they had had the cheek to oppose some Labour Party policies in the past!

LIES AND SLANDER

in order to defend their hopeless position, some supporters of the City Council - i.e. the news paper "Militant"- have descended to an unprecedented campaign of lies and slander against NALGO.

Continued on page 2 ......

NALGO cont. from page 1

"Militant" has constantly claimed that NALGO'S rank and file does not and will not support the boycott of the Race Relations Unit.The trouble is that every single NALGO meeting (including the Branch AGM) which has considered the issue, has voted overwhelmingly to support the boycott! NALGO'S action is also supported by Liverpool Trades Council, the City Council Joint Stewards Committee and the Regional Councils of GMBATU and TGWU. We have written to "Militant"

explaining that they appear to manage to keep getting the facts wrong and we wait with interest to see if they print the letter, and if they mend their ways. Since the boycott was imposed some Councillors have expressed the view that it would not be supported by NALGO members, and have publicly blamed NALGO for stopping the fight against racism. This is a sick joke. Since Mr Bond commenced "work" the boycott has been totally successful. And the old trick

of blaming the unions for every thing that goes wrong is something more suited to the Liberals than Liverpool's Socialist Council. The truth is that it is NALGO which is fighting alongside the black community to combat racism; it is theDLP and the City Council which refuses to listen to black people, refuses to allow them to address the Council, and calls in the police to have black people thrown down the steps of the Municipal Buildings when they protest.

Further blows to the Labour leadership followed at rapid intervals. The Liverpool Trades Council, an umbrella body for trade unions throughout Liverpool, endorsed the call to readvertise the post of Principal Race Adviser. The Joint Shop Stewards Committee, more significant given their role in co-ordinating the town hall unions, agreed that the post should be readvertised, having heard both representatives from the Labour leadership and the Black Caucus explain their positions. A similar pattern emerged throughout the trade union movement on Merseyside. The Black Caucus made every effort to attend wherever it could to explain what had happened in the interview for the Principal Race Adviser and in the subsequent sit-in, and totally unanimous support was achieved. The NUT, NATFHE and NUPE gave support in resolutions similar to the one passed by ASTMS:

> "This Region No. 6 Committee . . . gives its total support to the decision of the Joint Shop Stewards Committee of the Local Authority to boycott the appointment which has been made of a Principal Race Relations Adviser".

The most severe blows from individual unions came in the agreement of both the TGWU and the GMBATU to support the Black Caucus and NALGO position: these were, after all, Militant's power base and a failure to win these would represent a final seal of isolation to the political leadership. Yet the TGWU North West Regional Executive Committee stated that:

> "This Committee gives its total support to the decision of the Joint Shop Stewards Committee of the local authority to boycott the appointment which has been made of a Principal Race Relations Adviser".

And again the GMBATU Regional Committee made a similar decision, after hearing all sides of the debate:

> "The Regional Committee at their meeting of Friday, 16th November, 1984, decided to call on the Liverpool City Council to re-advertise the position of Senior Race Relations Officer. In doing so, the Regional Committee considered information submitted by the Leader of the City Council, members of the 'Black Caucus' and other relevant parties. After due consideration it was felt that there was a significant cause for concern. Branches are therefore advised that where they have delegates to other Labour organisations, i.e. Trades Councils, Labour Party CLP's etc., those delegates should be made aware of the policy of GMBATU."

A similar process of debate and resolution-passing took place in the branches and constituencies of the Labour Party itself. Here Black Caucus members attended as many Labour Party meetings as they could get access to, and three Constituency Labour Parties and eleven of the ward parties all opposed the activities of their leadership in trying to impose this appointment in the teeth of the trade union boycott and the black community opposition. Support also came from the Wirral District Labour Party.

> "This DLP in support of the City Council's JSSC, NALGO, NUPE, Riverside and Mossley Hill CLPs, calls on the Liverpool DLP to urge that the post of Head of the Race Relations Unit be re-advertised. It was the strong view of the meeting that the voice of Liverpool's black organisations should be listened to."

From a superficially unlikely source (given Militant's normal control over the Labour Party Young Socialists), support came from *Youth Action*, the North West Bulletin of activists in the Labour Party Young Socialists:

> "The actions of the City Council stand in stark contrast to the actions of the miners and their leadership over the past 12 months of the miners strike. The strength of the strike was the alliance that was forged between the miners and the most oppressed sections of our society including the black community. Liverpool City Council and the Militant Tendency have turned their backs on these lessons and have instead increased the divisions within the working-class in Liverpool, seriously undermining the struggle against Thatcher and the Tories. Youth Action must continue to fight to build the broadest possible support for the Black Caucus and the black community of Liverpool amongst youth both inside and outside the LPYS.

Again, support was given to the Black Caucus by other non-Militant strands within the Labour Party, including the Merseyside Co-ordinating Committee and its paper *Merseyside Labour Briefing* (Feb/March, 1985).

EDITORIAL
BRIEFING SUPPORTS BLACK CAUCUS

The furore surrounding the appointment of Sampson Bond as Principal Adviser in the Liverpool Council's Race Relations Unit has highlighted some of the worst failings of the politics which are presently guiding Liverpool District Labour Party.

Over three months ago, the disastrous actions of the leadership of the DLP opened up a massive rift between themselves and both the black community and the rest of the local Labour Movement. Under the guidance of supporters of the 'Militant' newspaper, the District Party first sanctioned the whole charade of Mr Bond's appointment, and followed this by the reaffirmation of the appointment and the reneging on the signed agreement to readvertise the post.

Since then the Party should have been using the chance to correct their mistakes. Instead, the splits have been widened to disastrous proportions.

Ranged against the position of the DLP are bodies which represent the widest possible spread of Labour Movement opinion. In the front line of this struggle are the NALGO members who gave overwhelming support to the boycott of the posts in the Race Relations Unit.

The list of organisations behind the re-advertisement is indeed an impressive one ranging from the Community Relations Council, through the TGWU and GMBATU Regional Councils, Liverpool Trades Council, numerous Labour Parties and extending as far as the Council's Joint Shop Stewards Committee. Significantly, a sizeable minority within the DLP itself have been consistently opposed to the tragic course of action which has been followed.

The response of the leadership of the DLP to this opposition has ranged from one unprincipled argument to another. Initially, great play was made of the alleged intimidation of Councillors Hatton and Lucock. The fact of the matter remains that Derek Hatton was quite content to confirm the contents of the agreement he signed when discussing the incident the following day. What happened to change his mind?

The leadership of the DLP made great play of the 'unrepresentative' nature of the Black Caucus and the 'alien' methods of its supporters. The allegations that the Caucus is unrepresentative were totally out of line with the way in which it had previously been recognised by the Party. Worse, only those with either a total ignorance of or antagonism towards positive race relations could envisage a predominantly white organisation using the word 'alien' in accusations against black people.

More recently, the DLP leadership has started on a new tack. Activists in the movement are expected simply to fall into line behind the leadership in preparation for a renewed battle over the City's finances. No concession is offered on the Race Relations Unit — we must simply forget the whole question while the 'Rates Roadshow' is relaunched.

This attitude is not good enough; the ethnic communities in Liverpool will not forget. Either the Labour Council will prove itself to be responsive to their hopes and needs or else it will continue to reinforce well-founded suspicions and mistrust.

The threat of the DLP being reported to the Commission for Racial Equality shows the depths to which relationships between the Party and the ethnic communities have sunk.

The Liberals and the Tories have called a special meeting of the Council to discuss the appointment on January 30. By that time the Labour leadership will have had ample time to find a more suitable post for Mr Bond. Failure to have done so will allow the bosses' parties to pose as friends of the black community. If that is allowed to happen, those who have supported the horrifically divisive course charted by the *Militant* supporters will only have themselves to blame.

The refusal of the DLP to listen to the ethnic communities when organising the Race Relations Unit is typical of the paternalistic and elitist attitudes of traditional Labour politicians. Until Socialists in the Party can change the clique currently leading Liverpool District Party, there is no real prospect of building links between the Party and black people and their organisations.

The strategy committee of the Merseyside Trade Union, Community and Unemployed Resource Centre, a significant Labour movement umbrella body with close links to the District Labour Party, also passed a very critical motion against the Labour leadership:

> "MTUCURC deplores the actions of the City Council in appointing a Race Relations Adviser against the wishes of union representatives and the representatives of Black Organisations on the appointments panel.
>
> We consider that this action undermines the Centre's work with trade unions and Black Organisations in the City.
>
> We therefore support the position of the Black Caucus and NALGO in calling for:
> 1. The re-advertisement of the post of Senior Race Relations Adviser.
> 2. A guarantee of no victimisation of those opposed to the position of the City Council.
> 3. The boycott of the unit until such time as when the post is re-advertised.''

The leader of the Merseyside County Council, non-Militant left-winger, Keva Coombes, had also made clear his opposition to the Bond appointment, as had Granby County Councillor, Margaret Simey. City Councillor Julian Clarke (a race relations lecturer) had made his unhappiness at the appointment clear, as did Cllr Dave Leach from Granby, who took part with Cllrs Coombes and Simey in the Rally and March called by the Black Caucus on the 14th November. However, despite the overwhelming lack of support from the trade union movement and the opposition of many of the Labour Party sections, both the District Labour Party and the Labour Group as a whole refused to back down from the impossible position that had been reached: they insisted on proceeding with an unworkable appointment, in which the Principal Race Adviser would be starting in a post boycotted by the whole of the local trade union movement and, as we shall see, by the overwhelming majority of the organisations in the black community.

In terms of assigning responsibility for the final decision to proceed with the appointment, we have made explicit the role of the core group around Militant in attempting to mobilise support for the appointment of their nominee Sampson Bond. But members of the Caucus felt much bitterness, not simply towards the well-known Militant group controlling the Council, but to the non-Militants, left, right and centre, who, at the end of the day, put up their hands both in the appointment committee, and then later in the Council chamber, to support this flagrantly unfair appointment.

Cllr John Hamilton, the leader of the Labour Group, was held to be particularly accountable, given his potential authority as Leader and his position as Councillor for the multi-racial Granby Ward, and his long association as a member of the Executive of Merseyside Community Relations Council. Granby Ward members were particularly criticised for taking few if any public initiatives to resolve the issue, as with the Abercromby Councillors, and for voting with the Party line when the crunch came, an explicit betrayal of the clear interests of the black community which should have led these councillors to refuse to endorse the appointment as these two wards contained a large proportion of the black population. However, Cllr Julian Clarke adopted a principled position by ultimately resigning his seat over the issue, whilst Cllrs Leach, Doswell and Lancaster did eventually make a protest when, on a subsequent occasion, the police were called in to clear black protestors from a Council meeting.

By and large, however, a key feature of Militant's control was the acquiescence of the Labour Group of Councillors as a whole in the excesses of their leaders, repeated time and time again throughout the period of Labour's rule, with the exception of the five 'right-wing' councillors who refused to endorse the illegal budget strategy, and the group of ten who, far too late in the day, accepted the need to break the unity of the Labour Group on the question of not recognising the Militants expelled by the Labour National Executive Committee in the early summer of 1986. Broadly speaking, Cllr Leach's increasing public criticism of Militant as Chairperson of Liverpool Labour Left has been the exception proving the rule.

A mixture of reasons lay behind this normally monolithic party front which ensured support at the Council level for every twist and turn of Labour policy and practice, including the obvious disaster of the Bond appointment. Militant itself had a sizeable group of councillors (estimated at twelve or thirteen) which provided a substantial core of support. As well as this organisational superiority, (for there was no other rival caucus of anywhere near this strength), Militant was ideologically supreme. Their simplistic workerism, anti-Toryism, anti-Liberal Party rhetoric, and general sectarianism provided a powerful magnet to the rather unsophisticated group of Labour councillors, both old-guard and new blood; there was also the ideology of 'democratic centralism', obeying the District Labour Party whatever its line, that had become accepted practice, together with the distaste for voting against the Labour Party (with the vilified Liberal or Tory opposition). It required a brave and determined councillor to stand out against this pressure, and such courage and confidence was largely lacking; there was also an element of sheer careerism — being a favoured and loyal member of the ruling group involved the perks of Committee office and other blandishments (including the continued support from the Militant machine for future nominations for Councillor); and finally there was no alternative ideological and organisational focus within the Labour Group, and barely one within the District Labour Party as a whole (see Crick, 1984).

The two versions of the speeches of the Leader of the Labour Group to the Municipal Conference in February, 1985, provide a fascinating glimpse into the internal practice of the Labour Party. The first version of the Leader's Report was circulated with the papers before the Conference. On the day of the Conference, a new speech had been substituted, and when a question was raised from the floor about the two speeches, Cllr Tony Byrne answered for Cllr Hamilton, the Leader, and said that the "Executive" had agreed to have it rewritten (presumably by Tony Byrne). The first version contained a number of hints at self-criticism and mistakes, referring implicitly but clearly to the conflict with the black community. The second version had removed all hint of doubt, self-criticism, references to faults and mistakes, and was all on the plane of triumphalist rhetoric alone. Sadly, John Hamilton brought no hint of his first speech to the Conference and fell in with the hackneyed complacency of his speech-writer — which is a symbolic statement of most of his period of leadership.

LEADER OF THE COUNCIL REPORT: MUNICIPAL CONFERENCE 1985 CENSORED VERSION

Note: All the passages in **bold type** were removed from the second version of the speech:

A very successful campaign was waged last year to bring to the attention of the people of Liverpool the financial crisis Liverpool City Council faced, and the unjust way in which Government grants were given to Local Authorities.

It was a successful campaign because it brought together a whole spectrum of city life to fight for a clearly defined cause. Not only Labour Party members demonstrated that unity, but there were trade unionists, Local Authority workers, housewives, teachers, community groups and many more sections of the public who are not normally active in political affairs who came out in support of our campaign. The enthusiasm penetrated the local media and the businessmen who are not usually sympathetic to Labour Party policies. These groups saw the truth and justice underlying our campaign.

The campaign itself generated its own driving power which intensified as the whole crusade developed. This was the reason why over 50% of the electorate voted at the Municipal elections in May. It was not the unity itself which helped to generate the enthusiasm. The cause was right and the people saw the basic truth in the cause. We were fighting to preserve jobs and services, to turn the tide of continual gloom about unemployment and economic depression. It gave people hope that something was happening, someone was trying to do something about the hopeless situation and, at last, a political party had come into office with a clear majority and spoke from the heart. At last a political party was not shouting political slogans without trying to fulfil promises.

What a remarkable advantage the Labour Party had. Here was a restyled party. A party with a radical policy, making promises and fulfilling them. An electorate being taken into consultation and decision making. A real challenge to an apparently unassailable reactionary Tory Government which resulted in a sizeable breach of their credibility and invincibilty. That was the position last July. What has happened since?

Instead of building up on these advantages there has been a succession of troubles which have sullied that image we had created. There are enough troubles already inherited from the Liberal/Tory regime which had to be solved. The question of a more efficient and effective housing repair system and a more regular refuse collection service were two services which are being tackled vigorously and, hopefully, we will soon see some positive results. We had come through most of the hurdles in creating a rationalisation of our secondary schools. A start in the regeneration of the worst of the housing needs were being tackled. These problems in themselves were enough to keep us occupied, together with the forthcoming budget problems, until the next round of municipal elections in the next couple of years time when we could make further gains by eliminating the Liberals for a lifetime.

We must face the fact that many criticisms levelled at the party are of our own making. We must recognise our faults and learn from them because our political enemies will be only too ready to use our mistakes for their own ends and remove us from office. We must have the courage to recognise these faults now and alter them while we still have a chance of keeping the political initiative and winning the next municipal election.

The faults stem from failures in our style of implementing our policies rather than mistakes in our basic policies.

Democratic socialism is for the improvement of human lives. It is centred around the need to free people from economic tyranny and oppression. It liberates them from the shackles and bondage of the market forces of the capitalist world. It elevates work and the role of the working person into one who is joining service to fellow beings, and removes the profiteering motives of a capitalistic society.

Our aim as a democratic socialist council must ensure that all our policies are based on this fundamental concept of socialism. The Labour Party believes that all people should have an equal chance in life. Our purpose is to provide employment for people and ensure that when we offer employment to someone it is on the basis that it is given to the person with the best qualities for the job. We reject totally the Tory approach of filling posts with their lackies because we believe in the dignity of labour and the need to build up each individual so that s/he is not subservient and dependent on favours to hold a position in society. In contrast to capitalism, socialism is built on trust and understanding and cannot be bought by money or acquired by favours. Socialism embraces human dignity, humbleness and the unity of mankind and rejects the acquisition of greater wealth and power for its own sake and overriding personal ambition.

Our policies on housing and social services, education and all the other aspects of local government affairs aim to ensure that people are not only relieved of personal anxieties and worries imposed on them by a capitalist system but that once those economic and social liberties are gained, they are free to live a richer and fuller life in other ways. **Our housing policies, and our policies for education and social services should be demonstrably seen to be desirable objectives by the people. If we create mistrust of our motives, then we should seriously question whether our methods of implementing our policies are wrong. Without the active support of the people and without their enthusiastic willingness to help us realise our policies, we will fail and we will be thrown out of office. Socialism has a human face as well as a determination to achieve its aims. We must never let our own personal zeal ride roughshod over the human needs and apprehension of others — socialism is based on uplifting of aspirations, and not suppression of others' initiatives and individualism.**

In a highly critical society where the press has the freedom to destroy any efforts of the people to rid themselves from the shackles of this society, it is important and necessary for councillors and leading members of the party to set standards which are beyond reproach. We do have the responsibility to show that our lifestyles are examples in the way in which we believe socialists living in a truly socialist society should behave. Everything we do must be related to and understood by the ordinary people living their everyday lives. They need to be taken into our confidence and just as we relate all our actions to the view and support of Labour Party activists, so we must ensure that the greater mass of the people are also taking part in the developments and feel involved in the decisions and the creation of a better Liverpool.

We succeeded with the Rates Campaign because we took the people with us and we were in tune with their basic needs. **We have created problems since because we thought if we are successful on one issue we would automatically be successful on every other issue. Now is the time for honesty and integrity to stand up and openly admit those mistakes, to recognise where those mistakes were, and we should have to assess our situation, to recognise that there have been some bad mistakes and ensure they are not going to happen again.**

We will soon be facing another round in the battle of safeguarding jobs and services and avoid massive rate rises. **Let us hope we can win this round by recapturing our zeal for basic simple socialist truths, and let us hope that where we have failed during the last twelve months we will have the sense and courage to put our mistakes right and have the modesty to learn from those mistakes so that our socialist council becomes a real people's council in every sense of the word.**

John Hamilton.
February 1985

Note: This text substituted, instead of the self-critical passages, the following orthodoxies:

There have been, as inevitably there will be in any large organisation, a multitude of problems and conflicts of views. In time and with perseverance these can be resolved. We have the usual distortion from the Tory Press which aims to damage the positive achievements we have made. These lies and distortions can only be countered by the active work of individual Party members in spreading the truth about our policies, and by our own publicity.

We succeeded with the Rates Campaign because we took the people with us and we were in tune with their basic needs. The people of Liverpool have been patient and have had to tolerate set backs in their social economic conditions. They have seen factories closing down, the run-down in trade, housing conditions getting worse and the ordinary basic services they need, such as a health service, allowed to deteriorate or disintegrate. They have a right to ask for a Council to speak on their behalf and fight for their basic needs. Against the onslaught from a reactionary Tory Government and the feeble compliance of a Liberal Council implementing Tory policies they looked to a new Labour Administration to give them new hope and better services. We would be failing in our duty if the Labour Council did not give a positive response to those wishes. We dare not fail them.

We gave that lead last year, not only to our city but to other cities round the country. We must succeed again this year and we must build on our past successes to ensure that Tories and Tory policies are never again predominant on the political scene on Merseyside. We can achieve those objectives because we have the right basic policies; we have the zest and stamina of a growing political Party in Liverpool and we have a cause which is just and reasonable. Let us go forward with the people and let us show that Socialism is not simply a theoretical ideal, but a practical and realistic aim for every man, woman and child on Merseyside. It is the only answer to the bankrupt economic politics of a capitalist system and it is the rock on which a better and bright future for Liverpool can be founded.

THE STRUGGLE FOR THE SUPPORT OF THE BLACK COMMUNITY

We have seen then that the Black Caucus was winning all the arguments and the votes in the Labour movement, except in the District Labour Party and the Council chamber where the Labour leadership consistently refused to allow the Caucus to put its case: Militant's subsequent crocodile tears over "natural justice" in their expulsions from the Labour Party have not impressed members of Liverpool's black community who have been consistently refused access to or physically ejected from crucial Labour Party meetings. Thus, at the final District Labour Party meeting which endorsed the Bond appointment, 6 December 1984, the only "non-Delegates" forced to leave the meeting were two Labour Party black women members.

The Caucus realised, however, that it was also necessary to win community backing for the stand that had been taken, particularly given the Labour leadership's attempt to dismiss the Caucus as "unrepresentative". A number of meetings at community level were held, in which Caucus members explained the stance that had been taken over the appointment, culminating in an enormous meeting at the Caribbean Centre on 17th October attended by at least two hundred people from the whole range of local community organisations. The meeting, after a full and lengthy discussion of the appointment procedure and the subsequent sit-in, unanimously passed the following resolution:

Caribbean Centre Meeting

"This meeting of the Liverpool 8 Community held in the Caribbean Centre on the 17th October, 1984, condemns the attempt by the dominant group within the Liverpool District Labour Party to impose on us as a totally inexperienced and unqualified person to the post of Principal Race Relations Adviser with the Race Relations Unit whose policies would have a direct effect on us.

This meeting gives its fullest support to the Black Organisations represented on the Black Caucus and the Race Relations Liaison Committee, in their opposition to this appointment. This meeting further condemns the District Labour Party in their decision to support a U-turn on the agreement made as a result of peaceful negotiations between the Black Community and the Labour members of the Interviewing Panel.

Finally, we demand that the agreement signed by Cllr Derek Hatton be reinstated in order to re-establish the Black Community's confidence in the City Council."

Black Linx

The meeting also agreed to establish a Black Caucus Support Group, to win broad public support for the boycott of the Bond appointment and to spread awareness of some of the broader race issues involved in this dispute; and also to organise a regular public lobby of the City Council which was maintained for many winter months outside the Municipal Annexe, as well as a public rally and march whose aim would be to try to persuade the City Council not to endorse the decision to go ahead with the Bond appointment.

During the month leading up to the rally and march of the 14th November, further formal support was won by the overwhelming majority of black organisations and race relations agencies in the city to demand the re-advertisement of the Principal Race Adviser Post.

Black Caucus Support Group

DEMONSTRATION

AGAINST THE APPOINTMENT OF SAMPSON BOND

ASSEMBLE

Wed. 14th November 11.30am Caribbean Centre, Amberley Street L8

The controversial appointment of Mr Sampson Bond to the positon of Race Relations adviser to the City Council's Race Relations Unit has provoked opposition from all sections of the Labour Movement on Merseyside. Black organisations have united with Trade Unions, Constituency Labour Parties, Ward Labour Parties and Community organisations to protest against the decision of six Labour councillors to appoint a totally inexperienced and unsuitable candidate to the most important post in the Race Relations field in this city.

For over two years, the Black Caucus - which is made up of representatives from Black organisations - has pressed the City Council to establish a Race Relations Unit. It was proposed that his Unit would conduct research into the problem areas of City Council service delivery (housing, social services, and education); would advise the Council on how to implement its Equal Opportunities Policy more effectively;to deal with complaints of racial harassment; to conduct anti racist training programmes for council staff and to promote policies for combatting racism within the various departments of the local authority.

Mr. Bond's appointment has aroused the anger of trade unions, Labour wards and constituency parties and many voluntary and Black organisations in the city. <u>Mr Bond was, undoubtedly, the least able, least experienced, least qualified and least suitable candidate for this post.</u>

The NALGO Union, whose observer was present during the interviews, have expressed their dissatisfaction with the decision to appoint Mr Bond. They have boycotted all work related to the Unit and have boycotted all other posts in the Unit. In an open letter to Labour Councillors, NALGO say "<u>If you proceed with this appointment, there will be no Race Relations Unit.</u>" They continue "The only conclusion we can draw is that some Councillors do not want - and never did want - a Race Relations Unit."

The City's Labour bosses have shown nothing but contempt for the views of Black organisations, trade unions, and a substantial section of their own party. All members of the Labour movement who are disgusted with the actions and behaviour of the Labour leadership on this issue must make their position known. We call upon Black people, Trade Unionists and committed anti-racists throughout the city to register their protest.

Join us in the **MASS RALLY** on Wednesday 14th November at 11.30a.m. at the Caribbean Centre, Amberley Street, Liverpool 8, and march with us on the **DEMONSTRATION** which will end at the Town Hall, Dale Street.

<u>**SHOW YOUR SOLIDARITY IN OUR STRUGGLE FOR JUSTICE**</u>

Thus, Merseyside Community Relations Council, the largest umbrella organisation with 60 affiliated organisations and 300 individual members, gave unswerving support for the stand taken by the Black Caucus.

MERSEYSIDE COMMUNITY RELATIONS COUNCIL CALLS ON ALL BLACK ORGANISATIONS TO BOYCOTT THE POST OF PRINCIPAL RACE RELATIONS ADVISER

On Thursday, 22nd November, a full quarterly meeting of Merseyside Community Relations Council endorsed a recommendation from its Executive Committee to boycott the post of Principal Race Relations Adviser and pledge total support to the Black Caucus, Local Authority Trade Unions and all Black Organisations in their fight to have the post readvertised.

MCRC is the largest Black umbrella organisation on Merseyside, with over sixty affiliated Black (and other) Organisations and over three hundred delegates on the Council, including delegates from Liverpool City Council, Knowsley Borough Council and Merseyside County Council. At a packed meeting Council members voted unanimously to support the Black Caucus and expressed grave concern about the appointment procedure that ignored the views of the democratically elected members of the Black Caucus.

MCRC delegates also mandated CRC Officers and staff to offer help and support to the Black Caucus, Trade Union Movement and Black Organisations, in the campaigning to readvertise the post but were most deeply concerned at statements by Liverpool District Labour Party and the appointed candidate that they did not support action programmes for Black people in Liverpool to redress the discrimination that has taken place over many generations, and debarred Black people from their rightful access to jobs and services. In this context the MCRC calls on Liverpool District Labour Party to adopt National Labour Party Policy and provide and support positive action programmes like ethnic monitoring for Black young people as part of the process of combatting racial discrimination and disadvantage in Liverpool.

In the light of the appointment and the lack of positive action policy from Liverpool City Council, delegates also demanded reassurance that existing provision for the Black community would continue to be recognised as a special need and that policy decisions in the pipeline like single sex education provisions and grant aid to Black organisations be honoured.

MCRC delegates also warmly welcomed the support the Black Caucus has received from many Trade Unions, Labour Party Wards, Labour Party Constituencies, the Black Section of the National Labour Party, Church Leaders and black and white community organisations in Liverpool and praised them for their courage in supporting and defending the Black Community in Liverpool in our struggle for racial equality.

Black Linx

The groups working most closely with the Liverpool born black community all gave their support at an early stage (South Liverpool Personnel, Charles Wootton Centre, Liverpool 8 Law Centre, Methodist, Liverpool Black Sisters). The attempts to make divisions in the black community by local Labour leadership claims that the "immigrant" organisations were not supporting the Caucus were refuted by other public statements made about the appointment:

Joint Statement by Ethnic Minority Organisations

"We the undersigned representatives of the ethnic minority organisations in the City of Liverpool have been watching with great concern the tragic events concerning the above appointment during the last six weeks. The public rallies, protest marches, intense lobbying, extensive media coverage, unrest among the community groups, growing tension among the political parties and trade unions and differences within the Liverpool Labour Movement on this issue have put back the race relations and community harmony by several years in the City which is proud of its multiracial and multicultural heritage.

Under these circumstances, we now strongly feel that the appointment of Mr Sampson Bond as the Principal Race Relations Adviser, due to his inexperience and lack of knowledge about Liverpool's deep rooted problems, will not heal the wounds after so much public disquiet in the City. The Race Relations Unit is not an established department of the Liverpool City Council; it is a fresh initiative for which full credit is due to the ruling group, but this City cannot afford to experiment with a novice as Head of the Department. We believe that skills and imagination of a seasoned practitioner in race relations is required to develop this Unit with his best abilities. We feel that this post should have been offered to a candidate with best qualifications, relevant experience and local knowledge.

In line with the impassioned appeals of the most reverend Bishops of the City and in line with the expressed opinions of the Leaders of all political parties in the Town Hall, we in our capacity as elected representatives of our respective organisations sincerely press upon the Liverpool City Council to reconsider their earlier decision and readvertise the post of Principal Race Relations Adviser in order to win the cooperation of the community at large and to ensure the ultimate success of the Race Relations Unit.

Joint Statement signed by:

Mr Ebrahim Yusif, Secretary, Somali Community Association.
Mr Marlon Cheung, Chairman, Merseyside Chinese Community Centre.
Mr Herbert Higgins, Secretary, Merseyside Caribbean Council.
Dr. D P Singh, Treasurer, Sikh Community Organisation.
Mr S A Khan, Secretary, Circle of Literary Friends.
Ms Shahana Salim, Secretary, All Pakistan Womens Association.
Dr S Pande, JP, Secretary, Hindu Cultural Organisation.

We see then that the Black Caucus was winning public support both from the Labour movement and from Black organisations. Other local influential voices such as the churches were also heard calling on the city to reverse its confrontationist approach towards the black community. To counteract the continued distortions of the stance by the Caucus on the Bond appointment, the Support Group produced various information documents and leaflets providing information about the appointment, the sit-in and the composition and work of the Race Relations Liaison Committee.

Efforts to popularise the activities of the Support Group included the production of Black Caucus badges, plastic bags and t-shirts: Gil Scott-Heron, black American rock protest singer and Red Wedge, the Labour Party popular music youth mobiliser, have performed on stage in Liverpool wearing the t-shirts, showing the ability of the Caucus to win a broad swathe of support. The National Labour Party Black Sections movement was won to the cause and leading Labour Party individuals such as Ken Livingstone (he condemned the "racism inside Liverpool City Council" and "attacked Liverpool Labour Chiefs for not giving black people more council jobs" *Liverpool Echo* 21 March 1986) and, eventually, Neil Kinnock came out in support of the Black Caucus.

(Some of the contradictions in the sources of support are worth noting: the aspirations of the Black Sections movement for an autonomous voice in the Labour Party reflect a parallel struggle to that of the Liverpool Black Caucus — yet on that issue, many of Labour's national leadership are in accord with Militant's opposition, on the identical grounds that Black Sections are 'divisive' — though, in fact, Militant has its own internal secret Black/Asian Section, whilst Labour's structure does have spece for womens', youth, trade union, and Jewish sections).

This initial part of the campaign culminated in a rally and march involving over 1,000 people from black and anti-racist groups, the trade unions, the churches, some sections of the Labour Party as well as many individuals concerned over this act of injustice by the Labour leadership towards the local black community. The Labour Group, however, continued on their pre-determined course of action, confirming the Bond appointment without allowing representatives from the march to give their point of view to the Council meeting.

To counter the public approval being won by the Caucus and the Support Group, the Labour leadership were mobilising their own forces to try and undermine the black organisations in the Liverpool 8 area. They produced leaflets for distribution in the area, and made house to house calls with a petition to support the Bond appointment, mainly through the use of the Militant/Labour Party Young Socialist network which was being reinforced by Militant activists drafted into the Liverpool 8 area.

BLACK LINX

Published by the Merseyside Community Relations Council.

December 1984   20p

Black organisations and
sections of the Labour
movement demonstrate
against the proposed
appointment of Sam Bond as
Principal Race Adviser for
Liverpool City Council.

SPECIAL ISSUE
RACISM
and the
CITY
COUNCIL

The City-wide Labour Party newsletter *Not the Liverpool Echo* was also used to try and win support for the Bond appointment and to continue the ideological attack on the black organisations begun at the District Labour Party, whilst the *Militant* newspaper carried regular reports praising Sampson Bond who in some of the more extravagant *Militant* writings was even being likened to Malcolm X as a hero of the anti-racist struggle!

The reality of the situation was, however, that Sampson Bond took up his post in a situation of universal boycott by black groups and trade unions, and was met on his first day of work by a mass lobby of protestors from the community and the labour movement. A strange Malcolm X figure that required a police escort to protect him from the black community he was supposed to serve, and to enable him to reach his office, and a strange socialist leadership that allowed the city's security staff to use the police to help them remove black leaders from the Council offices! This was not, however, an isolated incident and, as we shall see, a number of distinctly unheroic and unsocialist steps were still to be taken by Sampson Bond, his Militant associates and indeed the Liverpool Labour Group as a whole.

THE ABOLITION OF THE RACE RELATIONS LIAISON COMMITTEE

The existence of the Race Relations Liaison Committee, with the continued proof of the political legitimacy of the Black Caucus who were formal members of a Council Committee, was clearly a continuing source of embarrassment to the local leadership of the Labour Party. At the only meeting of the Committee that was held after the Bond appointment, the Black Caucus were able to secure a condemnation by the Committee for the Bond appointment through the strength of their votes when combined with those of the Liberal members of the Committee.

Race Relations Liaison Committee Resolution

The RRL Committee calls on the Labour Party to honour the agreement signed by Cllr Hatton on the 10th October. It states:

1) That the decision to appoint Mr Bond as the Principal Race Advisor be reversed.
2) That all the posts be re-advertised and appointment be made within a given time.
3) The Labour Party to speak publicly about their support for the Unit.
4) That there is no victimisation of the people who were involved in the peaceful action taken by the members of the Black Community.

In support of this agreement the RRLC also:

1) Deplores the claim of *certain* councillors, that they were the victims of violence and intimidation. The use of direct action, peaceful sit-ins

and occupations have been and always will be a tool of the trade union and Labour movements, and workers both black and white in their struggle against oppression.

2) We are concerned at suggestions that the Black Caucus on the Liaison Committee is unrepresentative, or dominated by so called 'factions' and we reaffirm the Council's support for the Black Caucus as representatives of Black Organisations, who live and work in Liverpool.

3) We deplore the suggestions that the action taken, as a result of the appointments procedure, by the Black Caucus and the trade unions was exclusively on behalf of the local candidates. This is not the case, the direct action was taken on the grounds that the appointee was not suitable for the post due to his lack of experience and knowledge, as well as his lack of political commitment, in terms of developing positive action programmes for black people in Liverpool.

4) We welcome the support of NALGO, the NUT, T&G, NATFHE, NUPE, ASTMS, the Local Authority Joint Shop Stewards, the Labour Party Wards, Abercromby, Granby, Arundel, Smithdown, Vauxhall, Fazakerley, Bootle and the Constituency Party at Riverside, as well as the Merseyside Community Relations Council and Black Organisations including South Liverpool Personnel, the Charles Wootton Centre, The Pagoda, the Circle of Literary Friends, the Somali Association, The Chinese Advisory Group, Merseyside Trade Union and Unemployed Resources Centre. We ask them to maintain a boycott of the post of Principal Advisor until such times as the post is readvertised and the proper *non*-discriminatory appointments procedure is followed.

5) We call upon the Chair and Deputy Chair of the Race Relations Liaison Committee to make a clear statement of support for the Black Caucus, trade unions and community organisations.

The Labour leadership of the City Council were quick to respond. With no consultation whatsoever, they formally suspended all further meetings of the Liaison Committee and then, once again with no consultation whatsoever with black organisations, with women's groups, with organisations for the disabled, with the trade unions or with the wards and constituencies of the Labour Party, and without bringing the proposal to the Municipal Labour Party Conference which was held in this period, the leadership introduced a proposal to scrap the Race Relations Liaison Committee and to replace it with an Equal Opportunities Committee to combine issues concerning black people, women and the disabled (no existing forum for the latter two interests existed at present).

The irony of the Labour Group itself abolishing the democratically elected forum of the City's Race Relations Committee whilst campaigning to prevent the Conservative Government's undemocratic abolition of the Merseyside County Council was not lost on the black community and its supporters. The proposal was criticised as nothing more than a divide and rule manoeuvre to provide a base for the disputed Race Adviser, and a speedy mobilisation of political forces was organised by the Caucus Support Group to try to dissuade the Councillors from implementing this proposal through the combined appeal of black groups, the trade union movement, women's groups and disabled organisations.

In the customary contempt for genuine consultation that has marked the general political approach of the city's Labour leadership, a mere six days "consultation" period was given between the letter from Cllrs Lafferty and Crowley sent to selected local organisations and the date when the formal ratification was due to be made of the proposal at the Council meeting on the 21st May, 1985. Nonetheless, all Councillors were sent a letter by the Merseyside Community Relations Council setting out the objections to the proposed change in Committee structure:

MERSEYSIDE COMMUNITY RELATIONS COUNCIL 16th May, 1985

Dear Councillor . . .

We are writing to you to express the deepest concern of our organisation at the plans to abolish the City's Race Relations Liaison Committee and to set up instead an Equal Opportunities Committee to cover issues of sex and disability as well as race.

Of course, genuine new initiatives by this Council to promote the interests of women and the disabled are necessary and would be warmly welcomed by us — but it is a sad fact that the Council's political leadership are attempting to use these legitimate concerns in a divisive way to silence the voice of the local black and ethnic minority communities that has been vigorously expressed since early 1981 by means of the Race Relations Liaison Committee.

Whatever claims are made, it is quite obvious that the real reason for abolishing the Race Relations Liaison Committee at a stroke and with no consultation, is that the Committee has at times been critical of Labour Party policies and practices including the disputed appointment to the post of Principal Race Relations Adviser. Thus this proposal is as undemocratic and as politically motivated as the plans of the Conservative Government to abolish the GLC and the Metropolitan authorities on the pretext of replacing them with "new, streamlined structures".

In the case of the Race Relations Liaison Committee, the pretext for abolition that is being offered is that the proposed new Committee will bring "greater powers" to race relations work: yet this is clearly contradicted by the proposal to replace a structure which gives equal voting powers to 12 black/ethnic minority representatives and 12 councillors, with a committee of 15 councillors massively outweighing the voices of the only 5 people who are supposed to represent the combined interests of women, black people and the disabled. Such a change will most significantly *diminish*, not increase, the potential influence and power that black people can exercise via the existing structure.

The proposal in fact goes on to acknowledge the unwieldy and unsatisfactory idea of lumping all the different concerns together in one committee, by suggesting that one of the first things the Equal Opportunities Committee will do will be to set up a Race Relations Sub-Committee! This is clearly an absurd suggestion given that there is a Race Relations Committee already in existence, which is the democratic and legitimate forum for discussing any possible improvements in the structure, powers or methods of local race relations work.

We must also point out that the proposed Equal Opportunities Committee is likely to be totally unworkable, given that beneath the surface statements it is clearly a political device by the Labour leadership to set up a base from which the disputed Principal Race Relations Adviser could operate. This is a further reason why this scheme will be unacceptable to black and ethnic minority groups in the City and to the trades unions who do not recognise this appointment, as well as to women's and disabled peoples' organisations who will not want to become embroiled in a structure set-up on such a divisive and disputed foundation.

The only sound basis for the progress of equal opportunities policies for all disadvantaged groups, to which we are totally committed, is for the setting up of any new structures for the interests of women and the disabled *in parallel to* not on the back of, the Race Relations Liaison Committee which should be immediately reconvened; whilst proposals for other structures should be discussed at length with the relevant womens'/disabled groups *before* rather than after any final decisions about them are taken.

We must ask you then not to go ahead with this proposal at the forthcoming City Council meeting, which will only exacerbate still further the current impasse over the city's responsibilities in the field of race relations and will bring the Council into conflict with yet more sections of the local community. We know that this point of view is shared by the majority of local black/ethnic minority groups, by women's groups, disabled organisations, trade unions and the churches. We hope you will take seriously this widespread concern and reconsider this misguided proposal.

Yours sincerely,

Gideon Ben-Tovim   Mohammed Anwar Herbie Higgins Ray Quarless
Chairperson, MCRC Vice-Chairperson   Treasurer   Secretary

Merseyside Womens Newspaper Autumn 1985

LIVERPOOL CITY COUNCIL is persisting with its plans to abolish the Race Relations Liaison Committee and set up an Equal Opportunities Committee in its place in spite of the fact that NALGO are boycotting the committee (refusing to type minutes etc). Although there was much talk of 'consultation' when the proposal was first made, this was soon abandoned when the massive scale of the opposition became clear. All the organisations and individuals listed here have denounced the proposal as "undemocratic and divisive" and have called for the city council to re-instate the RRLC and "to organise a process of full consultation with women's groups and disabled people's organisations BEFORE rather than after setting up new structures to deal with their interests".

Merseyside Community Relations Council
Methodist Community Centre
South Liverpool Personnel
Black Sisters Group
Liverpool 8 Law Centre
Third World Promotions
Merseyside Caribbean Council
Charles Wootton Centre
Black Caucus — Liverpool City Council
Race Relations Liaison Committee
Biko Housing Association
Black Mental Health Project
Merseyside Area Profile Group
Liverpool Black Media Group
Liverpool Black Organisation
ITEC (Charles Wootton Technology Centre)
River Avon St. Campaign
Mabel Achinihu Campaign
Circle of Literary Friends
Pagoda CC CAG
China Town Committee
Chinese Freemason
Wah Sing CCC
Liverpool Chinese Gospel Church
Pagoda CC and MCYA
Chinese Advisory Committee Group
Women's Centre
Pakistan Womens Association
WITCH (Women's Independant Cinema
House)
Lesbian Writing Group
Women and Ireland Group
Women's Reproductive Rights Campaign
Jewish Feminist Group
Merseyside CP Women's Group
Rape Crisis Counselling Service
Merseyside Women's Arts Project
Women's Technology Scheme
Merseyside Women's Paper
Feminist Discussion Group
Methodist Church
Cathedral Ecumenical Officer — Churches
Passionate Inner City Mission
Women's Equal Opportunities
Chairperson
Netherley Flat Dwellers Action Group
(Founder Members)

Homelink (Grierson St)
Homelink (Netherley)
Ujamma House Management Committee
TGWU 612
Chairperson Police Committee
Vixen Print
Riverside Constituency Labour Party
Granby Labour Party
Granby CP
LCVS (Liverpool Council Voluntary Service)
Merseyside African Council
Hindu Centre
Community Development Steering Group
Merseyside Skill Training
Liverpool Trades Council
Mossley Hill CLP
Princes Park & Granby Community Council
Sikh Community Organisation
St Margaret's Church
NUT
Labour Party Black Sections
MATSA
Riverside CLP
Picton Ward Labour Party
Bootle Ward Labour Party
Arundel Ward
Pirrie Ward
Vauxhall Ward
NALGO
ASTMS
NATFHE
GMBATU
NUPE
Somali Association
Wirral District Labour Party
CAB Netherley
Netherley Writers Workshop
Health Sub-Committee
L8 Business Training Centre (sight & sound)
NALGO Black Workers Group
Black Social Workers Project
Employment Resource Group
Merseyside Communist Party Women's
Advisory
WAVAW (Women against Violence against
Women

A petition signed by over 100 representatives of black and ethnic minority groups, womens' organisations, voluntary groups and labour movement organisations was also prepared for the City Council meeting.

> "We, the undersigned organisations, are opposed to the undemocratic and divisive proposal to abolish the Race Relations Liaison Committee of Liverpool City Council and to set up an Equal Opportunities Committee in its place. We call for the re-instatement of the Race Relations Liaison Committee and we call on the Council to organise a process of full consultation with women's groups and disabled peoples' organisations *before* rather than after setting up new structures to deal with their interests."

Thus a new broad alliance was forged between black community organisations and womens' groups, in the course of which a decision was taken to mount a joint lobby of the Council meeting due to ratify the decision over the new Committee structure.

Over 200 people took part in the lobby and 30 representatives were allowed in to observe the Council meeting. The organisers of the petition and lobby had requested permission from the Chairman of the Council to address the meeting, now standard practice if a 100-strong petition is presented in advance of the meeting, as was done in this case. The Chairman of the Council (Labour Cllr Hugh Dalton) however refused to allow anyone to speak to the petition and then when he also refused to give the floor to Granby Cllr Dave Leach who was going to oppose the abolition of the Race Relations Liaison Committee, the public gallery erupted in a spontaneous display of shouting and continuous protest at this undemocratic steam-rollering through of such an important and contentious issue.

Instead of trying to calm the situation by allowing a proper open debate on the issue, the Chairman then acted on what it transpired had been decided at the pre-meeting of the Labour Group and actually invited the police to remove the demonstrators — including a significant proportion of black women — from the Council chamber which they did with a show of great physical force.

This ultimate contempt for the norms and morality of acceptable socialist behaviour — a Labour Council acting in this premeditated way towards the Liverpool black community despite its long history of harassment at the hands of the police — was too much even for some of the Labour councillors, several of whom left the meeting in disgust. Policy authority Chairperson, Cllr Margaret Simey, also condemned the handling of the issue by the Labour councillors, saying "I wholly support" the dismay of local black people at their treatment (*Daily Post* 24 May 1985).

Despite the formal inauguration of the Equal Opportunities Committee, however, the strength of the opposition to its establishment has meant that the Labour leadership has never attempted to get the Committee to actually meet. Once again the firm alliance constructed around the Black Caucus ensured support from the whole of the voluntary sector and the labour movement and, once again, NALGO took up an official position to ensure that the Equal Opportunities Committee would not be able to function.

> This Branch notes with concern the establishment of a City Council Equal Opportunities Committee on 21st May for the following reasons.
>
> i)   The EOC replaces the RRLC with no prior consultation, nor the consent of the Members of the Race Relations Committee.
> ii) An Equal Opportunities Committee with only 5 Lay Representatives cannot represent the interests of all blacks, women and disabled organisations in City or the joint Shop Stewards Committee (particularly when compared to the previous Race Relations structure with 12 Representatives of black organisations and 4 Representatives of the Joint Stewards Committee).
> iii) There should be separate Committees for black, women and disabled interests as the same committee members cannot be equally knowledgeable and specialised in each interest.
>
> In addition, the agenda item for the City Council concerning the Equal Opportunities Committee was accompanied by a typed report by the Principal Race Relations Advisor recommending the establishment of an Equal Opportunities Committee. Therefore, this Committee agrees to boycott any work involved in the establishment and running of the Equal Opportunities Committee, including the calling and the Servicing of Meetings.
>
> This means that the Council's Equal Opportunities Committee is boycotted by the Branch.
>
> *NALGO Herald*

THE 'FRONT' ORGANISATION: MERSEYSIDE ACTION GROUP

With the failure of the attempt to set up a formal Council structure to give a legitimate platform for the activities of Mr Bond and to give a veneer of comitment to racial (and sexual) equality, Liverpool's Labour leadership now decided to give open support for the so-called 'Merseyside Action Group' as its chosen vehicle for local race relations interventions.

There is no doubt that this was a classical 'front' organisation, set up by the team of Militants imported into the Liverpool 8 area as nothing more than an operational base for Sampson Bond, for the advocacy of Militant's race 'policies' and for undermining established black organisations. After Bond was appointed, the influx of these Militant supporters into the Granby area had become a marked source of local tension. They were eventually attacked by local County Councillor, Margaret Simey, as "militant fascists" (*Liverpool Echo* 4 September, 1985), and their leaflets (resourced by their open use of the City Council's Militant-dominated Central Support Unit), local agitation and abuse of existing groups became a really destabilising force in the Liverpool 8 area.

In their joint article in *The Times* (1 October 1985) Archbishop Derek Worlock and Bishop David Sheppard of Liverpool criticised the:

> "dogmatic and divisive policies of the Militant leadership of the City Council. Perhaps the most dangerous example concerns the black community. The deliberate importation into the city of black members of the Militant Tendency from London brings a dangerous threat to the fragile but growing emergence of local black organisations. The appointment of Sampson Bond as Principal Race Relations Adviser was a needless affront to the Liverpool black community."

The situation was becoming so volatile that the NALGO observer on the Bond appointment was reported to have been physically assaulted by a leading member of Merseyside Action Group (*Liverpool Echo*, 13 October, 1985), and similar incidents were reported to have taken place. Thus to the political muscle of Militant (five full-timers were now members of the Granby Ward Labour Party) was added a dimension of widespread allegations of physical intimidation and aggression by their supporters. A real struggle for the streets was taking place which, at several points, nearly exploded into very ugly incidents.

One particularly serious point of tension took place at a very large meeting held in the Toxteth Sports Centre on the 16th September, 1985. Bond's supporters in Merseyside Action Group planned to disrupt and take over this meeting called to discuss the dispute with the City Council and use this to claim that the community was behind Bond rather than the Caucus. Many allegations were subsequently made that bribes were paid to local black people to bring Bond into the meeting and to protect him. These allegations have been supported by an affidavit (6 December 1985) sent to the Labour Party Inquiry into the activities of Militant in Liverpool and also by published statements of leading Merseyside Action Group members when they eventually resigned from the organisation.

AFFIDAVIT

1. I am a concerned member of Liverpool's locally born Black community.
2. On the evening of the 16th September, 1985, I was asked to meet Mr Sampson Bond who is the Race Relations Advisor for Liverpool City Council at the Municipal Buildings, Dale Street in Liverpool and I was aware that it was something to do with his attendance at the

Toxteth Sports Centre to address a meeting a couple of hours later that evening.

3. I did attend at Municipal Buildings at about 5.45 p.m. that evening and I was directed to an office on the top floor. I was introduced to a Mr D, a Mr E and a Mr L. There was also a black man by the name of R whom I knew came from Chester and was a businessman. Mr J and a number of people I know in the Liverpool 8 community were also there.

4. I was introduced to Mr D as "one of the bodyguards" and it was also mentioned by the person who introduced me that I and others would get £100 each as bodyguards. All this was a great surprise to me but I decided not to say anything at that stage but to listen and observe. I recall Mr D saying that there would be a slight problem about payment as red tape was involved and it had to be done unofficially.

5. I can describe the person introduced to me as Mr D as black and probably of Asian origin.

6. I saw Mr J looking at what I recognised as official documents giving financial details of the Charles Wootton Centre and the South Liverpool Personnel.

7. Mr L was present and I recall him asking what the response would be within the community to Sam Bond addressing the meeting and I recall him particularly mentioning specific members of the community who were opposed to Sam Bond's appointment. It was pointed out to him by some of the people I understood to have agreed to act as bodyguards that there would be considerable opposition to him attending the meeting. I recall L responding with the words "Some of our people will be tooled up". Just after this Sam Bond came into the room and asked if everything had been sorted out and arranged. Mr D responded by telling him that they were just sorting out the money problems but apart from that everything was in order. At that point I protested that everything that they were doing was immoral and informed them that I would have no part of it. I also mentioned to the people who had agreed to be bodyguards that they should be sure to get their money first because the people they were dealing with were untrustworthy. Sam Bond protested that that was not the case and Mr R informed the group that he was carrying £800 on him and he would lend that to Sam Bond "to pay the lads off". He said he would do that provided he had a guarantee that the money would be repaid to him. I recall a joint response to this from Mr D and Sampson Bond of "no problem". Mr D then said that the only problem that night was who received the money then and who would have to wait as the total amount needed was £1,200. At that stage I left the room in disgust.

8. I did attend the meeting at Toxteth Sports Centre later that evening and recall that three of the people who had been present at the meeting in Muncipal Buildings earlier on and had clearly been asked to attend as bodyguards came up to me and showed me the money they had received. They told me that they had each been given £100.

Blacks quit 'Militant' group

by Roger Ratcliffe

THREE officials of an ethnic organisation in Toxteth, Liverpool, have resigned because they claim the Militant Tendency was using them to recruit young blacks and teach revolutionary politics.

The Merseyside Action Group (MAG) was formed last September ostensibly to help the controversial race relations officer in Liverpool, Sam Bond – a Militant supporter – to win jobs for blacks with the city council.

But the three – chairman Robert Ellis, treasurer Dobbo Gibson and official spokesman Martin Jackson – have resigned, claiming their work was not so much opening job opportunities for blacks on the council and with other large employers as devoted to Militant Tendency work.

MAG was formed to give a fair hearing to Sam Bond, a black Londoner whose appointment in 1984 was hotly opposed by the established ethnic community leaders in Toxteth. Ellis, Gibson and Jackson joined MAG because, although substantial and was channelled into community groups by the government after the 1981 riots, many ordinary blacks did not reap the benefits and they wanted to give Bond a chance.

Among their specific allegations are:

1. Black members of Militant were imported to Liverpool from London by Bond to mastermind a Militant recruitment campaign in Toxteth. Two of them, Bob Leigh, an employee of the Militant newspaper, and Colin Defretis, a member, have shared a house with Bond at Huyton on Liverpool's outskirts.

2. Among MAG's plans is the acquisition with city council money, possibly £500,000, of a large building in Toxteth as a centre for blacks. The building earmarked for conversion is a former deaf and dumb centre. However, the three claim Militant talked about it being a "fortress" against police and fascist groups during future riots, where blacks could defend themselves.

3. Leigh and Defretis produced £1,200 to pay £100 each in cash to 12 blacks in Toxteth last September to act as minders for Bond when he tried to address a public meeting.

4. A city council minibus was used to take seven men from Toxteth to a conference of blacks at the Militant newspaper offices in London last November. The meeting was to set up a network of black groups, linked through Militant, to teach revolutionary socialism in immigrant areas.

Yesterday, Defretis said he rejected most of the allegations as hysterical. The three had misunderstood what had been said to them.

Defretis admitted he was a Militant member and that Leigh was employed by Militant. He said: "Of course, in discussion with black youths we have political perspective as to how black struggles unfold but at no time did we say that it should actually happen.

"We would say that it is essential for blacks in Liverpool 8 (Toxteth) to organise themselves against attacks on their community."

Bond said his main role was to secure jobs for blacks. He was not a Militant agent or member, although he was a sympathiser. Of the alleged "fortress" plan he said: "We wanted an efficiently run community centre, not just youths wasting their time on table tennis but a place for self-improvement."

MAG's chairman, Ellis, 31, a musician, said that initially jobs for blacks were promised but the talk "always moved back to Militant and teaching their politics on the streets, organising the blacks". Ellis was taken to the conference at Militant's London headquarters where, he claimed, he was told Liverpool was to be a link in a chain of black activists within Militant.

Several MAG officials were invited to join Militant discussion groups – the first step on recruitment. MAG's spokesman, Jackson, 32, an unemployed seaman, claimed: "It was always revolutionary talk. What they were getting into our heads was that it is not too difficult to seize power."

Duncan Baxter

Robert Ellis, left, and Dobbo Gibson:'Job creation became a Militant mission'

He said Leigh and Defretis talked of "mobilising" blacks in support of Liverpool city council's budget fight with the government and at other disputes in the city.

The treasurer, Gibson, 31, an unemployed car worker, said a study was in progress into the conversion of the deaf and dumb centre. He claimed: "I was left in no doubt it would be a breeding ground for Militant."

Sunday Times, 2 March 1986

Scandal of riot fortress on city rates!

Black leaders quit over 'Militant jobs con on the young'

THREE black community workers have quit over plans to establish a fortress for young revolutionaries in Toxteth.

The trio say that Merseyside Action Group — alleged to be a front for Militant Tendency — aimed to spend up to £500,000 on a fortress youth club.

Blacks there could defend themselves against police or fascist groups in the event of riots.

Merseyside Action Group was set up last year ostensibly to support the controversial race relations officer Sam Bond — a Militant Tendency supporter — to win jobs for blacks with the city council.

Now, Robert Ellis, chairman, Dobbo Gibson, treasurer, and spokesman Martin Jackson claim their work of securing jobs for blacks, took second place to Militant's recruitment campaign.

Liverpool Echo, 3 March 1986

Scandal of the riot fortress

From Page One.

They allege Militant blacks from London were imported to Liverpool by Sam Bond to mastermind the campaign, and that M.A.G. planned to set up the "fortress" youth club in Toxteth where black youngsters could be taught revolutionary politics.

They also claim a city council minibus was used to take seven men from Toxteth to a conference of blacks at the London office of Militant where a network of black groups to teach revolution was set up.

Martin Jackson (32) an unemployed seaman, said in an interview: "It was always revolutionary talk. What they were getting into our heads was that it was not too difficult to seize power."

By Andy Byrne

115

These allegations were confirmed in full by the relevations published in the *Sunday Times, Liverpool Echo* and *Daily Post* when the former officers of Merseyside Action group announced their resignations. The above statements contain damning evidence concerning corrupt practices involving Militant supporters and City Council staff. And yet the Council officials and Labour Party leaders have taken no action whatsoever to investigate these serious charges; nor significantly has any attempt been made by the Militants to take legal action against the former Merseyside Action Group members for making these statements, nor against the *Sunday Times*, the *Daily Post* and the *Liverpool Echo* who all published these accusations.

There were no limits to the smear tactics and dishonest statements that Merseyside Action Group and so through them, the Liverpool Labour Party leadership, were willing to use. Thus the response of MAG to the street disturbances of October, 1985, when serious incidents were averted by the actions of black community leaders (working closely with church leaders) in persuading the police to desist from highly provocative jeep manoeuvres on the pavements of Liverpool 8, was to try to actually blame the recurrence of police — black community tensions on the Black Caucus. A cross section of Black organisations sharply refuted this exact opposite of the true situation in a letter to the *Daily Post*.

Letter to *Daily Post* 5 October 1985

Dear Sir,

We the representatives of major community groups, race relations agencies and black organisations working in Liverpool, deeply deplore the statement referred to in your columns on 3rd October attributed to a group calling itself the Merseyside Action Group which accuses the Black Caucus of provoking the recent disturbances in Liverpool 8. To make such accusations at a critical time like this is an act of gross irresponsibility.

We should stress that far from provoking the situation, members of the Black Caucus and their respective organisations brought together a wider group including the Bishops, prison lay visitors, solicitors and doctors to try to negotiate with the police to defuse the situation and to provide support for people who were being intimidated, injured or arrested. As a part of this response, both the Community Relations Council and the Liverpool 8 Law Centre provided the emergency cover and were open until the police left the area and peace was restored to Granby Street.

We would like to commend all those individual people who offered support in the light of the heavy police presence and helped defuse the situation. We would also point out that the Liverpool City Council, the boycotted principal race relations adviser and the supporters of the so-called Merseyside Action Group took no part whatsoever in joining the collective community effort that was established to try to deal constructively with the situation.

Our organisations are appalled by this divisive and unprincipled attack on the integrity of the majority of the black organisations and race relations agencies in the City. We question the validity of the so-called Merseyside Action Group to speak on behalf of the whole community. No existing community group has been consulted or notified of the establishment of this group — they are clearly a self-appointed clique established by the Labour Party's Militant Tendency and appear to have their headquarters in the City's Municipal Annexe from where they clearly hope to establish a base for Sampson Bond. Bond's appointment has been boycotted by all accredited community groups in the city and the whole of the trade union movement.

Once again, the Militant Tendency are trying to discredit the long-established and democratically elected community groups and black organisations who have been working for many years to develop positive policies to combat racism and promote racial equality in the public and private sectors. The divisive tactics of the Militant Tendency and their supporters have been strongly condemned by prominent members of the Labour Party both nationally and locally and by the Roman Catholic and Anglican Bishops of Liverpool. The Community will continue to reject the sectarian policies of the Militant Tendency and their irresponsible attempts to undermine legitimate local organisations.

Finally, we would stress that the organisational representatives who have signed this collective letter would prefer constructive discussions with genuine members of this new grouping and indeed with anyone who is concerned to provide racial equality and justice in the City, rather than having to respond to destructive and scurrilous public polemic that Militant supporters obviously prefer.

Yours faithfully,

Liverpool Black Caucus
Merseyside Community Relations Council
Liverpool 8 Law Centre
South Liverpool Personnel
Liverpool Black Sisters
Charles Wootton Centre
Chinese Advisory Group
Circle of Literary Friends
Merseyside County Council Race Relations Office
All Pakistan Womens Association
Liverpool Arab Community
Merseyside Somali Association
Merseyside Skill Training Ltd.
Steve Biko Housing Association
Third World Promotions
Merseyside Caribbean Council
Liverpool Black Media Group

This then is the kind of organisation that Militant was fostering, with the collusion of the rest of Labour Group and the District Labour Party, to 'front' its activities in the Liverpool 8 area. Absurd claims were being made that this small and marginal group represented the ''real'' voice of their community, whilst the whole established network of accountable black organisations were branded as representing no-one. Yet, incredibly to most observers, Cllrs Hatton, Byrne and Lafferty proceeded on the 24th January, 1986, to appoint yet another Militant supporter to the Council pay-roll to provide secretarial support to the Merseyside Action Group. This appointment to work with a small and closed group with no known constitution or formal accountable structure was made with no officer report, without appearing on the Council agenda, without advertisement, job-description or interview and so breaking all trade union procedures. It was also made at a time when established black groups were all suffering from frozen vacancies, cuts in levels of grant and enormous insecurity and when indeed all the voluntary sector and much of the statutory service sector (especially education) were suffering severe cuts.

To add further insult to injury, it transpired that Cllrs Lafferty and Crowley (Chair and Vice-Chair designate of the non-functioning 'Equal Opportunities Committee') began to have secret meetings with Bond and the Merseyside Action Group under the heading of the so-called 'Joint Forum on Race Relations', a totally unofficial structure set up to try to provide yet another formal platform for Bond. The first meeting had also been attended by another tiny new Militant-supporting group, 'Merseyside Anti-Racist Campaign'. Once again, a rapid mobilisation of the Caucus allies was organised. An official NALGO boycott of all further meetings of the Joint Forum, and of the second unconstitutional appointment, was declared (23 January 1986) and a successful picket of the planned 'Forum' was mounted on 29 January which forced the meeting to be abandoned. The alliance was, however, unable to stop the appointment of Militant's second race relations worker to the Council staff, thanks to the enormous discretionary powers ruthlessly wielded by Cllrs Hatton and Byrne and as usual not opposed by a serious challenge in the Council chambers by the Labour Group members as a whole.

Nonetheless, it was proved time and time again that though Militant could secure jobs and other perks for their members and supporters (thus Bond supporters had been found a number of other jobs in the Council workforce through Militant control over the District Labour Party and Labour Group; in another notorious case a supporter had his suspension from a college course lifted on the personal intervention of the Chairman of the Education Committee), nonetheless they were severely isolated in any wider sense from the black community, the voluntary sector and the official trade union movement.

By contrast, the political support for the Caucus position on the Bond (and the second) appointment, and on the abolition of the Race Relations Liaison Committee had remained remarkably solid, despite all the means

Pickets block race forum

OPPONENTS of Liverpool race adviser Sam Bond claimed another victory last night after plans for a new group to meet were abandoned following a noisy demonstration.

Around 70 protestors, including members of town hall union NALGO, which has boycotted Mr Bond's appointment, the National Union of Teachers and members of the city's Black Caucus picketed entrances to the municipal annexe in Dale Street where the Joint Forum on Race Relations was due to meet.

A spokesman for the demonstrators said: "This so-called Joint Forum is an unelected, unofficial unaccountable body — yet it is being asked to consider a Code of Practice for combatting racism in educational establishments, despite the fact that the relevant unions and community organisations have not been consulted on the final draft of the document."

The protestors arrived at the annexe half an hour before the meeting was due to begin, mounting pickets at two entrances.

Doors to the annexe were closed by security staff and police arrived and kept watch.

After 40 minutes, a council employee who was to have attended the meeting emerged, saying it had been cancelled.

Mr Bond was not available for comment last night.

Daily Post, 30 January 1986

that had been used to undermine this unity. We have seen then how the alliance withstood the fierce ideological attack on black organisations ("self-seeking", "violent", "unrepresentative", "right-wing" etc.); the branding of trade unions and Labour Party members who supported the Caucus as "middle-class", "right-wing", "pro-Tory" or "pro-Liberal"; the financial bribery and coercion (compliant groups had much to gain from status, funding and security, whilst groups supporting the Caucus ran an enormous risk in terms of administrative retaliation through loss of grant or freezing of vacancies); and the undercurrent of physical intimidation and attack.

The depth of this support was illustrated in a very clear-cut way by the attempt of the Labour leadership to involve Bond in the series of appointments to the Chinese Social Work Unit. Despite the risk incurred of losing the whole initiative or jeopardising their own funding requirements, the representatives of the leading groups in the Chinese comnmunity that were due to take place in the interviews refused unanimously to go ahead with the appointments in Bond's presence. As a result of this stance, Bond was in fact removed from the appointments panel and the posts were eventually filled (9 May 1985). Again, a typical letter that appeared in the *Echo* (3 February 1986) from the three churches active in Liverpool 8, illustrates the broad basis of the public concern at the Liverpool Labour leadership's divisive and provocative activities in this area.

HORROR OVER RACE APPOINTMENT

We three clergymen represent the Methodist, Catholic and Anglican Churches in the Granby area of Liverpool 8. While we can only speak in our own name, we believe we express the horror of many in this area at the appointment, forced upon the City by a few ruthless cynical councillors, of Ms. Carol Derby/Dalton to the Race Unit.

People are well aware of the overall Militant design of infiltrating into all sensitive areas within the City Administration, Community groups, schools and trade unions, so that in the event of being ejected from office, Militant can effectively run or ruin the city as they wish.

There is no area more sensitive and where their aims are higher than in Race Relations, and the appointment of Sampson Bond now reinforced against the will of most Labour Councillors, by the appointment of Ms. Derby is an affront not only to us, to the Black Community, but to the whole city.

We believe that Militant is deliberately inciting anger among local residents by these very provocative appointments and by promoting the highly secretive, though high profiled Merseyside Action Group, along with unrepresentative supporting ''ethnic'' groups.

To reinforce the point there are more full-time Militant workers in the Granby Labour Ward than there are full-time Labour Party officials in the whole of the North-West.

We consider this to be very sinister and see it as our duty to inform the people of Liverpool about what is taking place.

David Copley, Peter Morgan, Colin Oxenforth, Liverpool 8.

THE OFFICIAL FALL OF THE MILITANT EMPIRE

For much of the period, the drama of the contest between Liverpool's Labour leadership and the black community was played out on the local stage alone. The situation became transformed, however, with the decision taken by Neil Kinnock, Labour's leader, to begin a process of ideological and organisational attack on the Militant Tendency. This was sparked off by the severe crisis the Liverpool leadership had precipitated through its attempted sacking of the entire Council workforce as part of its solution to the financial crisis faced by the city in the autumn of 1986.

The ongoing conflict with the black community had, however, already been brought to the notice of Mr Kinnock and his advisers through the publicity surrounding the Bond conflict, through the national Labour Party support that the Caucus had been developing particularly via the Black Sections network, and through the direct approaches the Caucus had made to Mr Kinnock to intervene in the issue. Indeed, Mr Kinnock eventually met personally with the representatives of the Caucus and the Support Group whom he referred to very favourably in his public criticisms of Militant activities in Liverpool.

> *Daily Post,* 22 October 1986
> **BLACK CAUCUS MAKES ITS POINT**
>
> Liverpool's Black Caucus got a sympathetic hearing from Neil Kinnock during a two and a half hour meeting at Liverpool 8 Law Centre last night.
>
> The Labour leader arrived an hour late to be ushered into the private discussions. When he came out he said what he had seen on his visit had alarmed him.
>
> "A lot of the information I have received has frankly alarmed me very, very much indeed.
>
> "I have had a discussion with representatives of the Black Caucus and indeed others from churches and others who are involved in the community in this area. They are serious people making serious allegations that I think have got to be followed through."
>
> Mr Kinnock said it was perfectly clear that in Liverpool people bore the greatest burdens of impoverishment and lack of opportunity, particularly blacks.
>
> "It is essential that the people's needs in this area are recognised, responded to in a way that will reduce and hopefully finish the alienation between the black and white communities which is developing, or the situation could become immense and dangerous for everybody concerned," he said.

In response to the pressure for a national Labour Party initiative on this issue, he attempted to send a team of 'eminent persons', including the nationally known equal opportunity specialists Herman Ouseley and Labour Councillor John Carr, to mediate between the Caucus and the City Council. The local Labour Party, however, who had refused on a number of occasions to meet with Black Caucus representatives, also declined to meet with the investigating team, and Derek Hatton wrote a vitriolic open letter to Neil Kinnock in which he attacked Mr Kinnock and his colleagues for meetings with the Black Caucus whom he described as "the enemies of the Labour movement" (*Liverpool Echo* 22 October 1986): an attack which the Caucus refuted in full in a subsequent article in the *Echo* (see over).

Despite Hatton's arrogant public attack on the Labour leader, the writing was clearly on the wall for him and his senior Militant colleagues, both from the National Executive of the Labour Party which set up an

The Black Caucus answers back

COUNCILLOR Derek Hatton (Liverpool Echo, October 22) accused the Liverpool Black Caucus of "organising physical attacks" on Labour councillors and party members. This is a total fabrication.

The appointment of Mr. Samson Bond lies at the centre of the race relations crisis that the Liverpool Labour Party have precipitated. A vendetta has been waged by Militant against the Black Caucus.

Who are the Black Caucus? At the end of 1980, the city council adopted a formal equal opportunity policy. A race relations liaison committee of 12 councillors and 12 local black representatives was formed. The community representatives (the "Black Caucus") have been regularly elected at annual meetings of black organisations.

The position of the caucus was reflected in the appointment committee for the principal race relations adviser, on which the caucus were allowed three voting members.

At the interview, Mr. Bond's lack of relevant qualifications and experience was obvious. He did, however, display a commitment to Liverpool Labour Party policies.

The predictable course of events was revealed when Mr. Hatton as chairman said they would only appoint someone who would "follow Labour Party policies".

He proposed Mr. Bond's appointment and, despite the caucus's strong arguments that any of the other five candidates would be acceptable but not Mr. Bond, the five other Labour councillors voted unanimously for Bond.

The caucus representatives and the Nalgo observer immediately walked out of the meeting because they felt this had clearly been a "fixed" appointment.

By the next morning, Nalgo had organised an official picket of the other planned posts in the race relations unit.

Derek Hatton's letter to the Echo last October calling Black Caucus "enemies of the Labour movement".

A sit-in in Mr. Hatton's office then took place involving members of local black organisations.

After several hours' negotiation, Mr. Hatton emerged to show his signed agreement that the principal race adviser post would be re-advertised. Mr. Hatton's promises proved hollow.

The next evening the District Labour Party branded the previous day's demonstration as "alien" to the Labour movement in an extraordinary display of double standards by the vehement supporters of picketing miners, Cammell Laird occupiers and other (mainly white?) "workers in struggle".

The Caucus became transformed overnight from elected and respected council sub-committee representatives to what has been called a "violent" and "unrepresentative faction".

Yet the sit-in had been entirely peaceful. There were no incidents, no arrests, no charges. The racist myth of "black violence" has been relentlessly pumped out by Militant propaganda ever since.

Councillor Margaret Simey, the Bishop and Archbishop of liverpool have all condemned the anti-Caucus leaflets and the activities in Liverpool 8 of the Militants imported from London to support Mr. Bond and Mr. Hatton.

Two Militant-inspired groups have been established: Merseyside Anti-Racist Campaign and Merseyside Action Group, for whom funding was recently proposed at a city council meeting.

A few local black individuals have formed an alliance with Militant,

but by and large the community has remained united despite the massive efforts to denounce the Black Caucus and to undermine or split local established black groups.

This ruthless approach of the Liverpool Labour Party has led to a major deterioration in race relations.

There are many more issues such as the abolition without consultation of the race relations liaison committee; recruitment (under one per cent of the council's workers are black); education (a long delay in issuing the code of practice to combat racism in schools, still no multi-cultural education unit, and an inadequate race relations co-ordinator scheme in the comprehensives); the cancellation of the River Avon Street housing project which was to be for black and ethnic elders and was to receive a 75 per cent grant from central government; social services—what happened to the "care of the elderly" report or to the black social workers project?; and the disregard shown for the Commission for Racial Equality's major housing recommendations regarding the inadequate and discriminatory practices that have occured within the city council's housing department.

A change of direction on race by the City Council critically overdue.

Gideon Ben-Tovim, Jeanette Bessman, Claire Dove, Liz Drysdale, Steve French, Irene Lynn, Ray Quarless and Protasia Torkington (Black Caucus members).

Liverpool Echo, 17 January 1986

Inquiry into Militant and the running of the District Labour Party shortly after the National Conference and from the District Auditor who had begun a process of surcharging and likely removal from office of the 47 Labour Councillors responsible for the delayed and illegal budget of 1985.

This dual intervention from outside Liverpool had at last put Militant on the defensive and provided the Caucus and their supporters with the prospect of the eventual vindication of their protracted struggle through the ultimate expulsion of their leading opponents from the Labour Party and from Council office. Given the range of oppressive and improper practices that the Caucus had experienced at first hand, the four Labour Party members in the Black Caucus felt it their responsibility to provide full evidence to the Labour Party Inquiry of the two 'fixed' appointments, the infiltration of Militant supporters into Liverpool 8, the allegations of financial improprieties and physical intimidation, the use of the police against the black community, the abolition of the Race Relations Liaison Committee, the persistent and provocative attempts to divide and rule the black community, and the general abuse of power and patronage by the local Labour leadership.

Members of the Caucus had included individuals from several different political parties or from none, but this had never caused the Caucus the slightest sectarian problem as all members put their commitment to racial equality and their responsibility towards the local black community as their essential priority, well before any notion of party loyalty.

Of course, the Caucus were criticised by Militant supporters for their "treachery" in giving evidence to the Inquiry, but Caucus members responded that it was Militant and the Labour leadership in Liverpool who had betrayed all socialist morality and principles in their unscrupulous attack on the black community, and that the national Labour leadership was acting perfectly correctly in trying to purge the Liverpool Labour Party of its rotten Militant core. The Caucus was, however, concerned that the collusion in Militant's racist policies and practices by non-Militant Councillors and the majority of District Labour Party members would be ignored through the national leadership's exclusive focus on Militant. One of the most virulent and powerful opponents of the black community and any form of positive race initiative was, as we have seen, non-Militant Cllr Tony Bryne, whilst the ultimate irresponsibility of Council Leader John Hamilton, was also being glossed over.

As the wheels of the Party and the legal machine were turning slowly but inexorably towards the official eclipse of Militant, their leaders still maintained right up to the end their vendetta against the organisations and individuals in the black community who had opposed them. Indeed there was a very real danger that, in true to the tradition of racial

Protest that went wrong

They walk alone

Councillors Tony Mulhearn (left) and Derek Hatton arrive alone for the start of the rally they did not join.

Liverpool Echo, 9 September 1985

Militant leave the field to the rest

By Janine Watson
Pictures by
John Davidson

IT was billed as Liverpool's greatest march against one woman and her Right-wing policies.

Instead it turned into a protest against a Left-wing man.

Race relations advisor Samson Bond stole the show and the anger that was meant to be directed at Mrs. Thatcher during Saturday's march against unemployment and social security cuts.

The man himself was not there—and neither were the people who appointed him. Liverpool's Labour leaders pulled out of the march when they knew the Black Caucus were coming.

Organisers were furious when Militant supporter Councillor Tony Mulhearn broke the news only minutes before the start of the march.

Shouting

Shouting shattered the silence as he and regional secretary of the TGWU Bob Owens faced each other.

Councillor John Hamilton sets off with the marchers, only to be recalled minutes later.

SUPPORTED BY MERSEYSIDE COUNTY COUNCIL, LIVERPOOL CITY
COUNCIL AND THE NORTH WEST T.U.C.

DEMONSTRATION
AGAINST
UNEMPLOYMENT &
SOCIAL SECURITY CUTS
SEPTEMBER 7th 1985

MARCH DETAILS: ASSEMBLE SEFTON PARK
AT 10.00 a.m.
RALLY AT ST. GEORGE'S PLATEAU
SPEAKERS: ERIC HEFFER, DEREK HATTON,
KEVA COOMBES, BETTY HEATHFIELD
TERRY THOMAS (South Wales NUM)
Plus other MPs & trade union leaders.

124

scapegoating, the black Caucus would be set up as the prime cause for Militant's ultimate demise. The Militant leadership in Liverpool were willing to take their grudge to the most anomalous conclusions: thus Cllrs Hatton and Mulhearn and the District Labour Party, including Cllr John Hamilton the Labour leader, even pulled out of a national Labour movement demonstration against unemployment and social security cuts on September 7, 1985, simply because members of the Caucus Support Group were organising a feeder march to start in Liverpool 8 and to subsequently join the main march on the route. Thus Militant's obsessive hostility to the Black Caucus had become elevated above all other socialist principles, such as class solidarity and opposition to unemployment, and this irrational blind-spot was, undoubtedly, one of the causes of their ultimate political exposure.

In the *Open Letter to Militant Tendency*, the Labour Party Black Sections National Committee have strongly condemned,

> "the damage done to the Black community by your White worker-favouring 'class reductionist' policies. Your most divisive stand to date has been the appointment of Sampson Bond — a man totally opposed to positive discrimination — to the post of principal race relations officer at City Hall.
>
> This decision was a slap in the face for a community which had stood four square behind the ruling Liverpool Labour Party's defence of jobs and services in the face of vicious attacks by the Tory government. Community groups like the Black Caucus, fully recognised by the Labour administration until they opposed the appointment, were ruthlessly denounced and purged from positions where they could influence council policy. This left the Black community who are eight per cent of the city's population and the most deprived without a strong voice in local government. After all, despite the fact that Black people have been settled in Liverpool for more than 200 years, there is not a single Black city councillor.
>
> Despite the boasts of your administration, the lot of Black people in Liverpool is no better now than it was under the Liberals. For instance, less than one per cent of the council workforce is Black. Of almost 3,000 poor people receiving meals on wheels, only nine are Black. Liverpool Labour Party's bitter opposition to positive discrimination led to you forcing the abandonment of the River Avon sheltered housing plan — mainly for Black elderly — despite an offer by the government to fund 75 per cent of the scheme. A report this year by the Commission for Racial Equality found that Liverpool Council's housing provision was pitted with examples of racial inequality. Among the observations was that Black people in the south of the city were virtually excluded from getting council homes outside the ghetto.
>
> Militant must use their influence positively to end racial disadvantage if you are to convince your critics both Black and White on the Left that your aim is not to remove autonomy among Black people and other oppressed

groups and replace it with subjugation to the views of solely your tendency in the Labour Party."
(*Black Sections Newsletter*, Spring 1986)

The persistent sectarianism displayed towards individuals involved with the Caucus or its support group was seen again in the period leading up to the Countil elections in May 1986 when the Militant controlled District Labour Party Executive refused to endorse a Black Caucus member as an "approved" member of the panel of potential Labour candidates. The person concerned was a prominent member of a number of black community and broader Labour movement organisations and campaigns, and this act of sheer political venom was the final catalyst that encouraged the emergence of an independent Black candidate to stand in the Granby Ward (the heart of Liverpool's black community). It should be noted that there was not a single black City Councillor in the whole 1980-1986 period, and not a single Labour Party black candidate in the 1986 local elections.

The eventual vote secured for the Independent candidate was, at 427, a very respectable figure given the electoral inexperience of both the candidate and his supporting organisations, the short period of the campaign and the normally poor showing of independent candidates in Liverpool. For Labour Party members and supporters, it was a matter of great concern that relations between the Labour Party and the black community had deteriorated to such an extent that a well known local black community worker should be standing on an overtly anti-Labour platform.

The damage done to the Liverpool Labour Party's standing in the eyes of many sections of the local black population over the whole period of this struggle has clearly been enormous and, indeed, Labour's handling of the race issue in Liverpool has shocked and alienated very many traditional Labour Party members and supporters. It remains to be seen, when the leading Militants and supporters, and the largely acquiescent body of non-Militant Councillors, are finally removed from local office through the surcharging process, whether the local Labour Party will be able to transform itself both in its general political approach and in its race policies in particular.

In this respect, it must be a matter of concern that Militant's formal demise has largely come about through external pressure and intervention from the Labour Party leadership and from the court cases brought by the District Auditor. The forces for change from within the Liverpool Labour Party have been weak and disorganised, and have shown (with a few exceptions) nothing like the determination, organisation and courage displayed by the Black Caucus and their supporters, who have been the most consistent and serious critics from the left of the policies of Militant and of Liverpool Labour Party.

If the non-Militant broad left in Liverpool, currently centred around the Liverpool Labour Left and the Merseyside Co-ordinating Committee, cannot quickly fill the vacuum left by the expulsions and surcharging to heal the breach with the black community as part of a process of socialist renewal in the local Labour Party, then Liverpool's black community will be quite justified in saying that the racism and the political bankruptcy of the Liverpool Labour Party is terminal; and that, despite the efforts of Neil Kinnock and his colleagues on the National Executive, certainly at local level the break with the Labour Party must be final.

If, on the other hand, Labour Party members can find the political vision, skill and leadership to begin a process of genuine political renewal, then an agenda is already available for rapid progress in the direction of racial justice and equality. During the life-time of the Race Relations Liaison Committee an enormous amount of policy development has taken place with respect to the Equal Opportunity Policy, and there is great potential expertise and coherence within the black community to bring about a series of practical changes that could have immediate impact on existing structures of racial inequality and exclusion.

All that is needed is the political will to use this expertise from within the Committee and the Community. It has been a profound shame to the Labour Party that the biggest obstacle to progress towards racial justice in Liverpool has been not the capitalist system, not Mrs. Thatcher's ultra-reactionary government and its massive assault on public spending in the inner cities, not the local Liberals, but the Labour leadership of the City Council and the District Party. The opportunity to repair this damage has been offered to socialists in Liverpool — if they fail again, they will not get another chance for a long time, nor in the authors' view will they deserve it.

It may, on the other hand, be the Liberal/Alliance which is elected into office when the bye-elections are ultimately held following on the House of Lords' decision on the expulsion from office of the surcharged Councillors. If that happens, then it will be the Liberals' opportunity to prove that they have also learnt the lessons of this period, and have the political will to bring about the committed programme for racial equality that they failed to deliver when they were themselves in office in the 1980-1983 period. In opposition the Liberals have made promises to rectify the current race relations impasse and to develop positive action initiatives. If they were returned to office, would their record in reality be substantially different from that of the Labour Council? A pessimistic reading of the whole period of the Equal Opportunity Policy would suggest that in practice, both the Liberals and the Labour Party have utterly failed to make serious inroads into the endemic racism in the City Council's recruitment policies and practices and in the delivery of Council services to the black community — and that there are too few signs of genuine anti-racist political commitment in any of the local political parties, left, centre or right. This is a profound indictment on the local political process and poses a major challenge for us all.

6 Conclusion: The Challenge to the Political Parties and the Whole Community

Although Labour was returned to power in Liverpool's municipal elections of May, 1986, the Militant dominated leadership had only a limited life span, with the expulsions from the Labour Party and the removal from office inevitably looming up on the horizon.

With the change in the personnel of Labour's official leadership and Council representatives, a major shift of Labour policy towards the black community was now a real possibility; whilst if the bye-elections caused by the surcharging of the 47 Labour councillors and their political exclusion were to lead to a Liberal dominated council, then a change of approach was assured — at least on paper.

At a public election forum held at the Liverpool 8 Law Centre under the auspices of Merseyside CRC just before the local elections, the Liberals produced a race relations manifesto that contained most of the demands currently being made by local black organisations: they would remove Sampson Bond from his post, restore the Race Relations Liaison Committee, reinstitute the River Avon Street sheltered accommodation scheme, fill the vacant Section 11 posts, introduce monitoring of housing allocations, promote positive action schemes and support black organisations suffering from staff cuts.

Whether or not the Liberals (their SDP allies are very insignificant in Liverpool) would actually implement these policies if they had the opportunity was, of course, another matter: their last period of office, as we have seen earlier, indicated some conflict between rank and file Liberal Councillors and their own leadership, with a distinct lack of commitment on race issues from the top frequently blocking the attempts of their more progressive junior colleagues to develop the Equal Opportunities Policy. However, the commitment by the Liberals to remove Bond and to restore the Race Relations Committee had been made public on so many occasions that it must be unlikely that they would renege on these very high profile proposals.

GRANBY FOCUS: RIVERSIDE LIBERALS (October 1985)

Working Together

No political party (including the Liberals), have tackled race discrimination effectively in the past. No political party has all the answers. Most importantly, no political party has the right to impose its views on the black community.

That is what the Labour council is trying to do. The symbol of their approach is the appointment of a race relations adviser with no experience

129

of race relations work, with no knowledge of the Liverpool black community, and with a belief (shared by the Militant run Labour Council) that positive actions are unnecessary to combat race discrimination.

That is why the Liberal party supports the boycott of Sam Bond and is committed to readvertising the post to get the best person for the job. A Liberal council will work with the black community through the Community Relations Council and other community groups to jointly agreed policies to combat racism and discrimination. The policies below, subject to the agreement of the black community would be implemented by a Liberal council as the first steps towards a fair deal.

First Steps To A Fair Deal
1. Remove Sam Bond and readvertise the post to get the best person for the job.
2. Restore the Race Relations committee with half the members being representatives of the black community with full voting rights.
3. Advisory representatives from the black community on all council committees.
4. Introduce monitoring of Housing allocations and Social Services to combat discrimination. Continue employment monitoring and increase schemes such as the black trainee housing managers scheme, using positive action principles.
5. Properly establish the race relations unit.
6. Ensure that all firms who get council contracts comply with a minimum set of equal opportunities guidelines.
7. Investigate funding for the River Avon St housing scheme and the Charles Wootton centre.

In the chaos developing within the Labour Party, there was no such clear-cut political commitment promised. There were, as we have seen, pockets of strong Labour movement support for the Caucus during their struggle with the now officially displaced Labour leadership and with the doomed City Councillors. This included several constituency Labour Parties and many wards, especially those where Black Caucus members or supporters were active, all the trades unions (on paper) and much of the voluntary sector: a substantial swathe, then, of support from Labour members and supporters. The non-Militant organisations Liverpool Labour Left and Merseyside Labour Co-ordinating Committee had been consistent in opposing the Militant stand on the Bond issue, as well as in supporting black community demands for positive action, monitoring and so on; whilst the harder left 'Rank and File' group, which emerged late in the day to provide an alternative power base to Militant whilst sharing most of its policies, was also in favour of the removal of Bond as part of a resolution of the dispute with the black community.

Given their breadth and size, these forces should have been able to ensure a shift of race relations orientation as the broader political conditions were changing. Demands were certainly being articulated within the Labour Party for a major break with previous practices — thus the following resolution gained support within several wards in the Riverside

Constituency, as a result of the pressure of Caucus members who had helped formulate the proposal:

Arundel Ward Labour Party Resolution (February 1986)

This ward is deeply concerned over the total break-down between the leadership of the Labour Party in Liverpool and the overwhelming majority of local black and ethnic minority organisations. This situation has arisen from the insistence of the Labour leadership on maintaining the untenable political appointment of Mr Sampson Bond, despite the nearly universal boycott by local black groups and the trade unions; from the undemocratic abolition of the Race Relations Liaison Committee; from the freezing of funds and posts to a number of local black groups; from the propagands war that has been waged on established black organisations and race relations agencies by a number of leading Labour councillors and in local leaflets or newsletters using the name of the Labour Party; from the attempts to split the local black community through fostering by various dubious practises the "front" organisation Merseyside Action Group; from the extraordinary decision recently made by Cllr Hatton, Byrne and Lafferty to appoint without interview, job advertisement and full Council approval, a second person on purely sectarian political grounds; from the continued resistance by the local Labour party leadership to carry out the array of practical and radical proposals urged by the Liverpool Black Caucus and other black groups on the City's leadership since 1983, in the fields of positive action employment policies and specific measures to combat discrimination and disadvantage and to meet the needs of the local black community and to eliminate all forms of racism.

In order to transform the current disastrous situation for the Labour Party and to provide a genuine policy base for any campaign to win electoral support, candidates for the Council and Party membership from amongst the local black community, we call on Riverside CLP to adopt the following as the core of its race relations policy:

1) The re-advertisement of the post of Principal Race Relations Adviser, along with the redeployment of the current post-holder to work not connected with the race relations field and then (and only then) the filling of the rest of the posts in the Central Race Relations Unit; and also, the termination of Carol Derby's temporary contract.
2) The re-establishment of the City's Race Relations Liaison Committee and the ending of current divisive manoeuvres to set up a spurious "Equal Opportunities Committee" or "Joint Race Relations Forum" in its place.
3) The filling of all the current government funded Section 11 posts which have been left unfilled by the current administration, despite their crucial importance as resources with which racism within council structures and services need to be combated:
eg *Multi-Cultural Education Resource Centre* (8 posts)
Further Education Race Relations Team (3 posts)
Ethnic Librarian Team (3 posts)
Ethnic Housing Liaison Officers (4 posts)
Various other posts in other departments, including social services.

4) The filling of vacant posts in black community currently left unfillled by current administration: e.g. Merseyside Community Relations Council (2 posts) and posts with South Liverpool Personnel, Somali Association, Methodist and others.

5) The development of a serious strategy for increasing black recruitment to the city council, which remains at a mere 1% of the city's work-force as a whole:

eg *the development of specific positive action training schemes in all Council departments.

*the strategic use of ethnic record-keeping and monitoring to set attainable racial equality targets for the Council as a whole and for each Department within the Council.

*close examination of all existing recruitment practices to eliminate direct and indirect discrimination and other forms of racial disadvantage.

6) Development of contract compliance unit to ensure, through a process of record keeping, monitoring and targets, that local employers develop practical equal opportunity and positive action schemes, and support local black businesses or co-operatives.

7) Development of and support for specific initiatives to ensure that any special needs of the local black and ethnic minority communities are met. eg Restoration of the River Avon Street Scheme, targeted towards black elderly currently heavily under-represented in Council sheltered accommodation, which was cancelled by Cllr Byrne and the local Labour leadership despite major central government funding for the project.

8) Implementation of major CRE report on housing allocations in Liverpool, which showed severe racial inequalities in housing allocations in the South City. Recommendations include:

a) development of system of record-keeping and monitoring (in association with black groups and trade unions) as a check on racial discrimination and to ensure that black tenants receive a fair share of housing resources;

b) appointment of specialist staff within housing department to ensure racially just housing policies and practices, as well as more active organisation of positive action training schemes and recruitment drive to increase black staff.

9) Development of more adequate codes of practice and policies on racial harassment and racism as disciplinary offense and also much wider consultation over recent Code of Practice on Racism in schools and colleges.

10) Taking of steps to ensure co-option of black community representatives on major Council Committees and Sub-Committees and onto governing bodies of schools and colleges and to all public bodies on which the Labour Party has nomination rights.

Finally as a means to support and monitor the development of this race relations policy:

11) The development of a Race Relations Advisory Group within Riverside CLP, to involve people active in the local black organisations and race relations agencies in advising the CLP on race relations issues.

Thus a similar set of practical proposals was now agreed within both the Liberal Party and sections of the Labour Party. Although it was likely that the Liberals would implement some of these commitments if returned to power, a major question mark still hung over the Labour Party because of the upheavals and power struggles emerging in the Party in the wake of the expulsions and the surcharging process. Whether the outcome of these internal battles would lead to the establishment of a non-Militant, broad left leadership of the District Party and the Council Labour Group remained to be seen.

It was possible that Militant, though purged of its leadership, could still regroup and reorganise its substantial base of support in Liverpool to retain its ideological and organisational grip over the District Party and Labour Group. On the other hand, though organisationally relatively weak, the broad left groups had a substantial potential mobilising power, given widespread Labour disaffection with many of the policies and practices of the Hatton-Byrne-Mulhearn leadership, and given the apparent commitment of the National and Regional Labour Party leadership that a solidly non-Militant group should take over the Labour Party in Liverpool.

A Liberal electoral break-through then, would open up the Council situation with respect to race relations policy, as would a real shift in power and direction in the Labour Party. The only resolution of the political crisis in Liverpool that would maintain the race policy status quo would be the persistence in office of a group of Labour Councillors dominated by the narrow, sectarian and racist world-view of Militant and their close allies and camp-followers, together with the perpetuation of a Militant controlled District Labour Party with its contempt for the massive grievances of the local black community.

If this political space opened up, then rapid steps could be taken to transform the situation. Through this long period of struggle, first with the Liberal and then with the Labour administrations, black organisations in Liverpool have developed a degree of coherence and awareness over the functioning of the local political structures that would ensure swift change given the slightest political will for progress towards racial justice.

The first steps that have to be taken are the reversal of the most blatant abuses of power. Sampson Bond has to be removed from his post as the essential condition for real political dialogue between the new Council leadership and the black community.

Secondly, the Race Relations Liaison Committee has to be immediately re-established, to provide a formal Council structure within which all issues of race relations can be debated between Councillors, officers and black community representative. Clearly, improvements may have to be made in the structure, functioning and powers of the Committee: but these have to be debated and developed in a democratic way, by means of the structure that had previously been agreed with black

133

organisations (ie the Race Relations Liaison Committee) rather than imposed unilaterally from on high.

Thirdly, the various frozen race relations posts within the local authority must be filled: this includes the readvertisement of the Principal Race Adviser post and the Social Services and Personnel Adviser, the Research, Training, Complaints and Clerical Officer posts in the Race Unit. Also the various agreed specialist teams and posts in education, further education, libraries, housing and social services have to be filled.

Next, the frozen posts and cuts in grant-aid to the various black community organisations have to be restored, as part of the Council's recognition of the valuable contribution made by the independent black sector and race relations agencies to the life of the City, to meeting community needs and to developing policy.

Again, a serious monitoring system, along with a system of racial equality targets must implemented, particularly in the fields of employment and housing; together with vigorous contract compliance initiatives to force contractors to adopt practical and monitored equal opportunity policies.

These are some of the initial steps a progressive Labour or Alliance (or hung) administration will have to take to begin to restore the black community's confidence in their genuine commitment to racial equality. These measures are only some of the preliminary building-blocks in terms of resources and structure that will enable the major overhaul of policy in every area of Council service delivery and employment practice to be followed. This radical transformation has been proved to be essential given the persistence of grave patterns of racial inequality in the Liverpool Council's employment profile (still less than 1% of its work-force are black) and in the delivery of services, with evidence of massive short-falls in social welfare provision for black people, huge racial disparities in quality and access with respect to council housing, and major racial disadvantages being perpetuated in education; as well as the persistence of more overt forms of racial discrimination, harassment and victimisation within arenas of Council responsibility.

This programme for radical change is by no means utopian. There is enormous expertise in the black community and its organisations in Liverpool, and amongst the black workers and other committed anti-racists within the Council work-force, to help tackle in a detailed, practical way, the task of reconstructing City Council policies and practices in a non-racist direction, and to devise positive action schemes and special needs programmes (where appropriate) to supplement mainstream changes. A very extensive range of local research and policy-oriented proposals is available (see Merseyside Area Profile Group, 1980; Lynn,

1982, Torkington, 1983; Ben-Tovim, 1983; CRE, 1984; MCRC, 1986 and many unpublished reports).

There is also a considerable body of knowledge of 'good practice' nationally available in the race relations field developed by black organisations and caucuses, by committed local authorities in other parts of the country particularly London, as well as in publications of the CRE and the Runnymede Trust, policy statements of professional bodies and trades unions, and in the official manifestos of the Labour and Alliance parties.

Within Liverpool, the Labour Party has demonstrated to those used to the indecisiveness of the previous decade of hung Councils that it is possible to bring about radical change through local Council structures, as in the housing and education initiatives. Whatever one's judgement of the policies adopted for Urban Regeneration or Schools' Reorganisation, they certainly showed the potential impact of sheer political will. Of course, the very ruthlessness of this determination had its negative aspect, in that the Labour leadership consistently refused to engage in genuine consultation with, or devolution of power towards, the people (employees or citizens) on whose behalf they were making and implementing these crucial decisions.

By contrast, the heart of any future local race relations policy must be a close dialogue with black organisations, and indeed with black community members not involved in the network of organisations. Certainly the experience of the last five years has resulted in the determination of the Black Caucus that adequate resources and structures must be found to keep the black community fully and regularly informed of relevant City Council developments, and to ensure maximum community participation in the decision-making process itself.

The Caucus have also learnt that there may be an enormous gap between the declaration of policy and its practical implementation: when access to the political process is restored, there must be constant pressure and vigilance towards Councillors, officers and town hall trade unions to ensure that the transgression, abuse or non-implementation of agreed policy does not recur as with the previous administrations.

The direct and influential involvement of Liverpool's black population in City Council affairs, whether as Councillors, senior staff or trade union officials would, of course, play a crucial role in this process of monitoring and implementing race policy and practice and preventing subversion or resistance. But until this has been achieved, the role of the black organisation representatives on the Council's Race Relations Committee will remain crucially important. Proposals to co-opt black representatives on to all Council Committees, within departmental advisory groups and working parties and on to governing bodies of schools and colleges, will be an important means of enhancing the black community voice in the policy-making and decision-taking process. To be fully effective, those initiatives require more adequate mechanisms to be developed to ensure the democratic accountability of Committee activists to the wider grass roots community, whose autonomous organisations must have a central part to play in any future race equality strategy and structure.

Of course, the reality of Liverpool's massive current financial problems may be used as an excuse to justify inaction on most of the necessary changes. But the resources required to genuinely begin the long haul of redressing the balance of racial injustice in Liverpool are not necessarily that enormous. Much of the initial outlay on staffing and capital resources has already been allocated to Liverpool in substantial levels of unclaimed Central Government grants, whether through Section 11 or the Urban Programme. Many of the changes, such as in the nature of representation and co-option, or in the insistence of a racial dimension in all Council reports are purely administrative (though highly political) and require little outlay. Some of the race equality mechanisms (eg monitoring and targets, or contract compliance) can have significant effects for small costs. Some of the required changes involve a redistribution of existing resources to ensure that the black community gets a more equitable share of the Council's employment opportunities and of service delivery.

But where substantial new resources will have to be found, this must be accepted by politicians and public as necessary to ensure that Liverpool's black and ethnic minority population receives at last a measure of the social justice and equality denied them for so long and with such particular virulence over the last two years of Labour rule.

It must be stressed that though the experiences recounted in this book are clearly unique — Liverpool is the only City Council in Britain controlled by Militant — they raise issues of far wider political relevance. The black population in this country is still encountering massive racial discrimination and disadvantage in every institutional sphere, as recent national research reports such as those from the Policy Studies Institute (Brown, 1984) and the Runnymede Trust (Newnham, 1986) have consistently demonstrated.

Clearly, then, central and local government have failed and are continuing to fail to develop adequate policies, practices and resources to secure racial equality and justice, despite the relatively small size of Britain's black population (approximately 4% of the society as a whole) and the substantial accumulated knowledge of the steps needed to greatly improve the situation.

Some of the factors highlighted in this book are certainly present in other local authorities (albeit perhaps in less extreme form) and contribute to the overall context of continuing, indeed, worsening racial injustice: the colour-blind ideologies of local politicians, whether based on socialist, liberal or conservative principles, which lead to a refusal to adopt positive action measures to redress the balance of proven racial inequalities, or the reluctance to accept the need for special provision to meet particular needs of black and ethnic minority communities; the defensiveness and conservatism of professional council officers which makes them resistant to any serious acknowledgement of well founded charges of overt or institutionalised racism and obstructive of changes to mainstream policies, practices and services in an anti-racist direction; the protectionism of trades unions which makes them refuse to surrender cherished privileges or traditions even when they are known to discriminate against the black population; the political sectarianism, the paternalistic authoritarianism, the narrow parliamentarist mentality, as well as the sheer crude racism, with which the local council power-elite prove unwilling to genuinely open up local government structures to ongoing black community involvement in decision-making; the smug complacency with which token and cosmetic gestures (an Equal Opportunity logo, a black appointment, a toothless committee, marginal funding for a small project, or anti-racist rhetoric) are used to inhibit the development and implementation of concrete and comprehensive action programmes and policies.

These, and many other of the tendencies illustrated in Liverpool, can be reproduced in town halls throughout Britain. Of course there are exceptions, particularly though not exclusively in London Labour authorities, with progressive developments in some of the provincial city and county councils as well. And, of course, central government must bear great responsibility, particularly the current Conservative regime (though previous Labour governments had a generally poor record too on race and immigration issues) in not developing decisive and comprehensive race equality measures and in creating a financial and ideological climate that discourages and undermines positive local race initiatives.

But these factors should not be used to excuse local government for its general failure to use its still very substantial powers, discretion and resources from making the enormous contribution to racial equality of which it is capable: and, in returning again to Liverpool, we have seen how the Council leadership has been able to develop certain new initiatives in other areas despite its chronic financial difficulties caused by cut-backs in funding instigated by the Conservative Government.

At the end of the day, we are not simply talking about financial resources (important of course though they are) but about the political will and commitment to ensure that the highest priority is given to the development of appropriate structures, policies and practices to promote the cause of racial equality.

That is the responsibility of us all: the current Militant dominated Labour leadership of Liverpool City Council have demonstrated their total indifference to this concern, with their policies of malign neglect and negative action towards the local black community. A new set of councillors are soon to be elected. If after the mass of evidence of all-pervasive racial inequalities, after the explosion of grievance in the streets of Liverpool 8 in 1981, and the signs of further disorders in 1985, after the sustained attack on local black organisations and neglect of black interests during this last period — if after all this, Liverpool's political leaders still cannot find the commitment to restore genuine dialogue with the black community and to take whatever positive action is required to start redressing the balance, then there can be no prospect for social justice and peace, for 'freedom and fairness', in this city.

We hope then that the publication of this book will make some contribution to stiffening the resolve of political activists, council officers, trade unionists, community workers, civic and church leaders and, indeed, all citizens, that the bitter political struggles outlined in these pages will not have to be fought again.

Bibliography

Ben-Tovim G. S. (Ed.)   (1983) *Equal Opportunities and the Employment of Black People and Ethnic Minorities on Merseyside* — Conference report and resources pack. (Merseyside Association for Racial Equality in Employment and Merseyside Area Profile Group).

Ben-Tovim, G. S., Gabriel, J., Law, I. and Stredder, K.
  (1986) *The Local Politics of Race* (Macmillan).

Black Linx   (1984) *Racism and the City Council* — Special Issue, December — 1984 (Merseyside Community Relations Council).

Brown, C.   (1984) *Black and White Britain: the third PSI Survey* (Policy Studies Institute/Heinemmann).

Brown, W.   (1983) "Unemployment and the Black Community on Merseyside", in ed. G. Ben-Tovim, *Equal Opportunities and the Employment of Black People and Ethnic Minorities on Merseyside*, (qv).

Brown, W.   (1986) "Race, Class and Educational Inequality in Higher Education" (unpublished paper, Liverpool University, Sociology Department).

Caradog Jones, D.   (1940) *The Economic Status of Coloured Families in the Port of Liverpool*, (Liverpool University Press).

Colonial People's Defence Association   (1952) *Report of Activity 1950-1952* (CPDA).

Craggs, S. and Lynn I. Loh   (1985) *A History of the Chinese Community*, (Merseyside Community Relations Council).

Crick, M.   (1984) *Militant* (Faber and Faber).

Fletcher, M.   (1930) *Report of an Investigation into the Colour Problem in Liverpool and Other Ports*, (Liverpool University Press).

Fryer, P.   (1984) *Staying Power* (Pluto Press).

House of Commons Home
    Affairs Committee   (1980) Race Relations and Immigration
                                      Sub Committee, Session
                                      1979-80, *Racial Disadvantage:*
                                      Minutes of Evidence together with
                                      Appendices, 14th October 1980,
                                      Liverpool (HMSO).

Humphrey, D. and John, G.
                                 (1972) *Police Power and Black People*
                                         (Panther).

Inner Area Study Consultants,
    Liverpool   (1977) *Change or Decay?* (HMSO).
Julienne, L.   (1979) *Race Riots: 1919*, (Charles
                                        Wootton Centre).

Law, I. G. and Henfrey, J.
                                 (1981) *A History of Race and Racism in*
                                         Liverpool 1660-1950, (Merseyside
                                         Community Relations Council).

Liverpool Black
    Organisation   (1980) Memorandum to House of
                                        Commons Affairs Committee,
                                        Racial Disadvantage, (HMSO) (qv).

Liverpool Education
    Committee   (1973) *Meeting Their Needs*, Working
                                        Party on the Educational Needs of
                                        the Children and Liverpool Born
                                        Descendants of Immigrants
                                        (Liverpool City Council).

Liverpool Social Services
    Department   (1983) *Care for the Elderly in Liverpool 8*,
                                        (Liverpool City Council).

Liverpool Youth Organisation
    Committee   (1968) *Special but not Separate*,
                                        (Liverpool Council for Voluntary
                                        Service).

Lynn, I. Loh   (1982) *The Chinese Community in*
                                        Liverpool — their unmet needs
                                        with respect to education, welfare
                                        and housing (Merseyside Area
                                        Profile Group).

McNabb, P.   (1969) "Integration in Liverpool: a
                                        Definition of the Problem", in
                                        Parliamentary Select Committee
                                        on Race Relations and
                                        Immigration, *The Problems of*
                                        Coloured School Leavers.
                                        Evidence taken at Liverpool,
                                        March 1969 (HMSO).

Melish, I., Ben-Tovim, G. S. and McNabb, P. **(1972)** "Patterns of Discriminatory Behaviour by Police and in the Courts Facing the Locally Born Black Population in Liverpool", in Parliamentary Select Committee on Race Relations and Immigration, *Police/Immigrant Relations*, Vol. 2, H.M.S.O.

Melish, I. McNabb, P., and Ben-Tovim, G. S. **(1973)** "The Relevance of 'Race' to Education Opportunity in Inner City Liverpool" in Parliamentary Select Committee on Race Relations and Immigration, *Education*, Vol. 3, HMSO.

Merseyside Anti-Racialist Alliance **(1978)** *Merseyside Against Racism*, (First Annual Report of MARA).

Merseyside Area Profile Group **(1980)** *Racial Disadvantage in Liverpool — an Area Profile*, (evidence to House of Commons Home Affairs Committee, Racial Disadvantage, (HMSO) (qv).

Merseyside Community Relations Council **(1980)** Memorandum to House of Commons Home Affairs Committee, *Racial Disadvantage*, (HMSO) (qv).

Merseyside Community Relations Council and Liverpool Black Caucus **(1986)** *Racial Discrimination and Disadvantage in Employment in Liverpool*, Evidence to House of Commons Select Committee on Employment (Merseyside Area Profile Group).

Nalgo Herald **(1985)** *Race Boycott Goes On* — Special issue, vol. 2, no. 9, July 1985 (National Association of Local Government Officers, City of Liverpool Branch).

Newnham, A.	(1986)	*Employment, Unemployment and Black People*, (Runnymede Trust).
Race Relations Board	(1976)	*The Leaving of Liverpool* by D. Mills (North West Conciliation Committee).
Richmond, A. H.	(1954)	*Colour Prejudice in Britain — a Study of West Indian Workers in Liverpool*, (Routledge and Kegan Paul).
Rooney, B.	(1981)	"Active Mistakes — a grass roots report", in ed. J. Cheetham, et al *Social and Community Work in a Multi-Racial Society*, (Harper and Row).
Rooney, B.	(1982)	"Black Social Workers in White Departments", in ed. J. Cheetham *Ethnicity and Social Work* (George Allen and Unwin).
Rooney, B.	(1983)	"Liverpool City Council Social Services Department: Race Related Employment Issues — a Summary and Discussion", in ed. G. Ben-Tovim, *Equal Opportunities and the Employment of Black People and Ethnic Minorities on Merseyside*, (q.v.).
Sommerfeld, P.	(1979)	"The Black Social Work Project", in ed. M. Marshall, *Social Work in Action*, (B.A.S.W.).
South Liverpool Personnel	(1978)	*Black Prospects — a report on the job prospects of Liverpool-born Blacks*, by C. Watts (SLP).
Torkington, N. P. K.	(1983)	*The Racial Politics of Health — a Liverpool Profile* (Merseyside Area Profile Group).

The Runnymede Trust

The Runnymede Trust is a registered educational charity set up in 1968. Its objectives are the collection and dissemination of information and the promotion of public education on immigration and race relations. This is done in a number of ways:

- An information service which provides information on race and immigration.
- A reference library of books, pamphlets and press cuttings which may be used by prior appointment.
- A monthly bulletin, *Race and Immigration*.
- Publication of pamphlets and papers on matters of current interest and concern.
- Seminars and meetings.

Other publications of interest

Different Worlds — racism and discrimination in Britain (P. Gordon and A. Newnham) £2.50 (new revised edition)

Employment Unemployment and Black People (A. Newnham) £1.50

Racial Violence and Harassment (P. Gordon) £1.50

Racism and Discrimination — a select bibliography 1970-83 (P. Gordon and F. Klug) £3.50

Routes or Roadblocks — consulting minority communities in London boroughs (U. Prashar and S. Nicholas) £2.50

The New Right — image and reality (Ed. N. Deakin) £2.50

Please add 15% for postage and packing (minimum 25p)

A full list of publications and details of subscriptions to *Race and Immigration* are available on request.

Runnymede Trust
178 North Gower Street
London
NW1 2NB

01-387 8943

Merseyside Area Profile Group

This group consists of members of the Sociology Department at Liverpool University working, in association with local racial minority organisations and individuals, on investigations into racial discrimination and disadvantage on Merseyside and on the development of positive policies for the promotion of equality of opportunity and the elimination of racism. Other publications of the Group:

1. **History of Race and Racism** (I. Law and J. Henfrey, for MCRC)
2. **Racial Disadvantage in Liverpool** — an area profile (eds. G. Ben-Tovim, V. Brown, D. Clay, I. Law, L. Loy, P. Torkington)
3. **The Chinese Community in Liverpool** — their unmet needs with respect to Education, Social Welfare and Housing (I. Loh Lynn)
4. **A History of the Chinese Community in Liverpool** — (S. Craggs and I. Loh Lyn, for MCRC)
5. **The Racial Politics of Health** — a Liverpool Profile (P. Torkington)
6. **Equal Opportunites and the Employment of Black People and Ethnic Minorities on Merseyside** — (ed. G. Ben-Tovim, for MAREE)
7. **Race and Housing in Liverpool — a Research Report** (I. Law, G. Ben-Tovim et al for CRE)
8. **Racial Discrimination and Disadvantage in Employment in Liverpool** (Merseyside Community Relations Council and Liverpool Black Caucus).

Further information and orders from:

Merseyside Area Profile
Department of Sociology
University of Liverpool
Liverpool
L69 2AF

051-709 6022 Ext. 2649